REMARKABLE

⇥ UTAH ⇤

WOMEN

SECOND EDITION

CHRISTY KARRAS

TWODOT®

ESSEX, CONNECTICUT
HELENA, MONTANA

*To Mom and all the other women
who have been my mentors.*

———•◦•———

A · TWODOT® · BOOK

An imprint of Globe Pequot, the trade division of
The Rowman & Littlefield Publishing Group, Inc.
4501 Forbes Blvd., Ste. 200
Lanham, MD 20706
www.rowman.com

Distributed by NATIONAL BOOK NETWORK

British Library Cataloguing in Publication Information available

Library of Congress Cataloging-in-Publication Data

Names: Karras, Christy, author.
Title: Remarkable Utah women / Christy Karras.
Description: Second edition. | Guilford, Connecticut : TwoDot, [2022] | Series:
   Remarkable women | Includes bibliographical references and index.
Identifiers: LCCN 2022025716 | ISBN 9781493066841 (paperback) | ISBN
   9781493066858 (epub)
Subjects: LCSH: Women—Utah—Biography. | Women pioneers—Utah—Biography. |
   Women—Utah—History. | Utah—Biography.
Classification: LCC CT3262.U8 K37 2022 | DDC 970.7209792—dc23/
   eng/20220712
LC record available at https://lccn.loc.gov/2022025716

♾™ The paper used in this publication meets the minimum requirements of American
National Standard for Information Sciences—Permanence of Paper for Printed Library
Materials, ANSI/NISO Z39.48-1992.

CONTENTS

———◆●◆———

ACKNOWLEDGMENTS

Surely, to-day, whoever inflicts an additional volume upon a long-suffering public, ought to be able to set up an unassailable plea in justification thereof.

—CORNELIA PADDOCK, *IN THE TOILS*

Anyone writing about the past relies on the work of many, and this project made me appreciate all the more those who help write the stories of their times—whether they be newspaper reporters or private citizens keeping diaries.

Then there are the people who carefully preserve and share those accounts, including historians who put it all together and make sense of what it means. Their work is all the more valuable in traditionally neglected areas like women's history.

In the years after I wrote the first edition of this book, Utah has seen an explosion of people investigating, sharing, and celebrating women from all aspects of its history. This made my job easier—although it did make it difficult to narrow down the list of which women to include in this edition!

Michele Welch spearheaded the Utah Women's Walk, which collects and publishes interviews of and about Utah women. Within a few short years, she has built an invaluable resource for anyone interested in women's stories.

In 2020, to celebrate the one hundredth anniversary of the nineteenth Amendment and the 150th anniversary of Utah Territory giving women the right to vote, a group of volunteers formed the nonprofit Better Days project. Its educational resources include biographies of notable Utah women, many from traditionally underrepresented backgrounds.

Several entities in particular made my research possible and deserve recognition and huge thanks.

The Utah State Historical Society's helpful staff made working at its archives a pleasure.

A joint project of Utah's academic and research institutions, the Mountain West Digital Library maintains an invaluable electronic database of statewide documents and photos, which are now easily available to the world.

I am indebted to the very helpful special collections librarians at Utah State University's Merrill-Cazier Library, the University of Utah's Marriott Library, and Brigham Young University's Harold B. Lee Library. They patiently answered my many questions and went the extra mile to locate resources.

The Marriott Library also hosts the Utah Digital Newspapers Project, a searchable database of papers large and small, old and new. No more microfilm!

The Salt Lake City Public Library has a lovely collection of resources on Utah and Mormon history.

The Church of Jesus Christ of Latter-day Saints welcomes all kinds of researchers, and its mostly volunteer staff cheerfully handles all kinds of requests.

I am grateful to Jennifer Toomer-Cook and Darren Parry for their help in telling their mother's and grandmother's stories. I hope I have in some small way done them justice. Thanks to my patient and capable editors at The Rowman & Littlefield Publishing Group, Inc.

Finally, thanks to my family and friends, and especially Bill, for help, encouragement, and putting up with me in general when I was paying more attention to the book than I was to you.

INTRODUCTION

The historians of the past have been neglectful of woman, and it is the exception she be mentioned at all; yet the future will deal more generously with womankind, and the historian of the present age will find it very embarrassing to ignore women in the records of the nineteenth century.

— EMMELINE WELLS, "SELF-MADE WOMEN"
WOMAN'S EXPONENT, MARCH 1881

As Emmeline Wells knew, women have not always gotten their due. That's both a shame and an opportunity for those of us who now have a chance to help right the balance.

The history of Utah's women is the history of Utah. We are sometimes inclined to think of past women's lives as full of drudgery, but in reality, women have always had to be multifaceted and multitalented. The subjects of this book are only a sample of Utah's many accomplished women.

It is impossible, in an overview such as this, to give more than a fleeting look into any woman's life. But I hope to give a taste. Each woman in this book also represents something larger than herself.

I hope this book, as others have before it, goes a little way toward putting Utah's women into the larger context of the West. The people who live in Utah are as diverse as the state's many landscapes, but Utah sometimes gets painted with an overly broad brush. Books about the West sometimes avoid Utah, as if the surrounding mountains literally cut the state off from the rest of the world.

But women in Utah are like women anywhere. And in some ways Utah's culture actually made it easier for them to succeed. Its unique social structure meant that a woman could rise on the basis of her intellect and ambition, not her circumstances of birth or class or even sometimes race—things that could make it difficult for women elsewhere to become prominent or influential.

It's not possible in the scope of this book to note every worthy woman, as much as I wish I could. That's partly because we simply don't know enough about some of them. Hundreds of years of civilization before white settlers arrived undoubtedly produced many extraordinary women. Navajos, for example, had a largely matriarchal society in which women could do pretty much whatever they were capable of achieving.

Many of the women we know of from Utah's Native American tribes are mythical figures, such as the Navajos' Spider Woman, who taught the ancient people to weave. But without written records, generations of identities are mostly lost in time.

It's easier to study Mormon women's lives because church members have always been encouraged to keep diaries and family histories. Mormons—that is, members of the Church of Jesus Christ of Latter-day Saints—were diligent about documenting their own history. But they were less concerned with the histories and cultures of the people whose world they entered.

(*One practical note:* I have generally used the term "Mormon" to refer to members of the Church of Jesus Christ of Latter-day Saints, since it's less cumbersome yet still recognizable by both members and people outside the faith.)

Other groups later arrived and set up a counterculture that did as much to encourage woman leaders as the Mormon church did. Believers and nonbelievers were part of a web that interconnected culture and government as well as the faithful. Their struggle to learn to live together makes for some fascinating episodes.

Many of these women knew each other. One of the church leaders that Jane James petitioned for equal treatment as a Black member of the church was Angus Cannon, husband of Martha Cannon. Martha worked in the women's suffrage movement with Emmeline Wells (though the two were more rivals than friends). John Bransford, brother of Susanna the "Silver Queen," was mayor of Salt Lake City when madam Belle London ran the city's experiment in government-sanctioned prostitution.

Although they lived diverse lives, these women had many things in common. For one thing, all of them persevered through tough circumstances. Writing about them, I was struck by the many times they had to pick themselves up, dust themselves off, and get back to work after some kind of significant hardship.

They had plenty of experience overcoming the heartache that goes along with saying goodbye to a loved one. Many of them were married more than once, having lost husbands to death or divorce. (Out of the seventeen women in this book, only five had just one husband; four of them were married three or more times.) Many of them had children who died before them.

While some ended up wealthy or at least well-off, none of the women in this book came from privileged circumstances, and all of them faced economic trials at one time or another. They found ways to support themselves and their families, often with surprising success. They showed great pluck when it came to getting something done. Many of them didn't accomplish their most notable achievements until the second halves of their lives.

As even these brief notes about their personal lives attest, notable women also tended to be unconventional, willing to stick their necks out and do the unexpected. As all successful people do, they displayed a determination and work ethic that kept them going when someone told them no.

All this makes the women in this book quintessential citizens of the West. As much as any man, they show that here it was possible to carve a new path and stake out a unique identity. In doing so, these women serve as an example that will continue to inspire.

PATTY SESSIONS

(1795–1892)

PIONEER MIDWIFE

Read just a few entries in Patty Sessions's diary and you'll get a good idea of how she lived. Take, for example, a few days in the winter of 1855. Working as a midwife, she helped a woman through a difficult delivery of twin babies. She hired a man to build a fence around her prized fruit orchards. She knitted a pair of mittens, a rug, a dress, and two pairs of stockings. She conducted a meeting of the charity she headed, then gave another group an educational lecture on raising children.

She visited friends, took care of a sick woman who was brought to her house, and distributed some vegetables she had preserved from her garden. A few days later, she was called to care for another pregnant woman—and that evening she attended dance lessons.

At the time, Patty was a vibrant sixty years old.

Patty Sessions lived for nearly a century during some of the most tumultuous times in Utah and American history. More than forty years of her life survive through her meticulous diary, now preserved in archives of the Church of Jesus Christ of Latter-day Saints, commonly known as the Mormon church. But she was famous in Utah long before anyone read her diaries, and her writing would not have been interesting to historians or admirers if she hadn't been such an inspiring woman.

All her life Patty never waited or asked for help from anyone: If something had to be done, she did it herself, whether that meant delivering a woman's baby or driving a wagon across the plains on the trek to Utah. Her life embodies the can-do spirit that fueled all pioneers to make the arduous journey westward and create new lives for themselves and later generations.

Patty Sessions worked in her orchard, healed the sick, and taught school well into old age.

Patty was born in Maine in 1795, when much of the present-day United States was still a mystery to white settlers on the East Coast. Her father was a cobbler and her mother a seamstress. Married at seventeen to David Sessions, she almost immediately started to help her mother-in-law, who worked as a midwife. She didn't get much schooling but loved to write and was always curious about the world around her.

That curiosity may have been one reason she listened to missionaries preaching about modern-day revelations God had delivered to a young man named Joseph Smith from upstate New York. Already a devout Christian, Patty was baptized into the Mormon church in 1834, four years after Smith founded it, and persuaded other family members to join the next year. In 1837 they moved to Missouri, where the Latter-day Saints hoped to form a community of believers.

By this time Patty had already given birth to seven children, four of whom had died; she was pregnant again when the family made the difficult trip by foot and wagon to Missouri. At forty-two she was showing the stamina that would serve her in busy decades to come.

A year later, violence erupted between Latter-day Saints and Missourians, and more than two dozen people were killed in bloody skirmishes. Upon hearing about the fighting, Missouri's Governor Lilburn Boggs issued an "extermination order," giving the Mormons a choice between death and exile. Running from mobs of suspicious residents as well as the state militia, families quickly packed up what they could carry and moved to Illinois, leaving their new homes and farms behind.

It was winter and no one was prepared for such a journey. Patty Sessions trudged through deep snow, ice-encrusted rivers, and mud that sucked at her boots and skirts. She did all this without enough food, carrying her young daughter, Amanda, in her arms as she walked. Sometimes she had no shelter but a tent. At night she would try to keep herself and her baby warm. But the baby was sick for much of the journey. Amanda would die soon after Patty's family reached the new settlement of Nauvoo, Illinois.

By the early 1840s Nauvoo was a thriving town with about 12,000 residents, Mormon and otherwise—about twice the population of Chicago. As one of the church's early converts, Patty Sessions was close to Joseph Smith and considered him a modern-day prophet.

Joseph Smith was spiritually married to a number of women, including Patty. Mormons believed being "sealed" in their temple formed a bond that lasted beyond death. Since women who were sealed to church leaders anticipated living in the afterlife with the men chosen by God to lead His people on Earth, it was a great honor to be chosen as one of them. Both Joseph Smith and Brigham Young married women who were already married to other men, which meant men like Patty's husband might be blessed with multiple wives—but one of his wives could also be "sealed" to a church president.

Patty formed a lifelong circle of friends with a group of elite Mormon women she would later call "Brigham's girls" or "Heber's girls" (many of the women were married to church leaders, including presidents Brigham Young and Heber C. Kimball).

It was while they lived in Illinois that Patty Sessions began keeping a diary, in a simple notebook a friend had given her. She was fifty-one years old and had already established herself as a vital member of her community. Spelling, punctuation, and clarity were not Patty's top priorities. Her diaries were filled with smeared ink, crossed-out words, and crammed handwriting. It was an account she wrote for herself, not for posterity.

She wrote things as they happened, giving the account a lively sense of immediacy. In brief stream-of-consciousness daily entries, she recorded even the most mundane details of her life, including the time she spent washing, sewing, or gardening. Those details, together with more thoughtful commentary and items about the people she knew, make for an engaging record of one well-known woman's life and times.

Mormons' happiness in Nauvoo was short-lived. In 1844 violence erupted again between Mormons and residents of surrounding communities. In retaliation, the Mormon militia tore down the presses of an anti-Mormon newspaper. Joseph Smith and his brother Hyrum were arrested and killed by a mob while in jail, and Brigham Young took over as head of the church.

The Mormon pioneers knew they were not safe in Illinois or any place where they could incite an unsympathetic local population. They decided to head west, across the Rocky Mountains and into the Great Basin. They didn't know much about their new home, except that other white pioneers hadn't deemed the arid, mountain-ringed valley worthy of settling. What is now Utah was then part of Mexico (it would become part of the United States in 1848, after the Mexican–American War). "We started for a resting place, we knew not where," Patty wrote.

Patty Sessions and her family helped form the "Big Company," which arrived in the Salt Lake Valley shortly after the first group of settlers in July of 1847. As the family's leader (several of her children and their families came west with her), she drove and maintained her own wagon—evidence of her independent and tough-minded spirit.

She slogged up to twelve miles or more a day through prairie grass and over rocky hills in a region with no roads. Sometimes, at the end of the day, she had to turn around and retrace her steps to minister to a sick traveler or help a woman give birth. She once delivered three babies in six hours while the convoy moved westward. Sometimes the women had babies after walking or riding for miles earlier in the day. Patty's diary records one instance where a woman continued on the trek for thirteen slow miles *after* she went into labor.

Sometimes Patty went for days without sleep. When she did sleep, it was often with aching muscles and raw hands. On her fifty-second birthday, she helped a woman give birth, went to a small party her friends had for her, then tended to another two women that same night.

Patty worked under difficult circumstances, with almost no equipment or medication. She didn't even have access to the fresh herbs that were the foundation of her treatments. Sometimes, the most she could do was keep patients clean and warm—and pray they would get better. She and her own children were often sick. "I have never felt so bad as now, but I am not discouraged yet," she wrote, laid up in the back of the wagon during one long illness. But she pushed forward in her typical determined fashion. "My health is poor, my mind weighed down, but my trust is in God."

"Mother Sessions" was known not only as a skilled midwife but as a healer with the ability to minister to both physical and spiritual needs of the sick. She would do a "laying on of hands" for healing and give religious blessings. Her diaries record many instances of "speaking in tongues," which was common for healers in many religions at the time. Joseph Smith had encouraged this role, quoting the biblical book of Mark: "Signs follow all who believe." He felt this applied to women as well as men.

It was also common for women to preside over their own church meetings, which were a mixture of religion and socializing. In one women's meeting, organized by her friend Eliza R. Snow, "they spoke in tongues, I interpreted, some prophesied—it was a feast," Patty wrote, with obvious satisfaction. At another meeting Patty "blessed Sister Christeen by laying my hands upon her head and the Lord spoke through me to her great and marvelous things." Many of those roles would later be designated specifically as men's responsibilities, but Patty's acts show how powerful women were in the church's early years.

Though she was one of Joseph Smith's many "celestial" wives, Patty was less happy about the idea of her husband taking other wives. When David married his second wife, Rosilla, the two strong-willed women fought often. Their sour relationship drove a wedge between Patty and her husband.

Months of Patty's diary entries complain about Rosilla and tell of Patty's sadness when her husband seemed to be favoring his other wife. Writing was an outlet for this woman who wasn't used to feeling helpless. Patty detailed Rosilla's "saucy tongue," her refusal to do chores, and her threats to take David for herself. "Have had another long talk with Rosilla. She says she will not receive any advice from me, she will do as she pleases," Patty wrote in October of 1846. Her diaries make it clear how hard it was for this whirlwind of a woman to share her life and her husband with someone she disliked so much. Then again, Patty's forceful personality probably would have made it hard for her to back down to any sister wife.

Rosilla eventually gave up and returned to Nauvoo. Even though David was angry that Patty had driven Rosilla away, Patty must have been secretly pleased at her victory. When David Sessions took a third wife, Harriet, Patty tried to make peace with the arrangement, drawing on her deep well of inner strength. Like other women of her time, she believed that polygamy was a commandment of God, and she relied on her faith to get past the heartache.

She also turned her energy toward her many outside enterprises—always a source of satisfaction and self-confidence. When she arrived in Salt Lake City, she set up a home surrounded by fenced orchards she carefully tended (people in Utah still grow the Sessions plum, which she first cultivated). She sold fruit most of her life; she also grew herbs for the poultices and emetics she used for healing. She kept notes on payments from her patients—as well as the times when they couldn't afford to pay and she didn't ask them to. She kept meticulous records of her finances, including money owed and repaid on loans to family, friends, and the church.

She was shrewd in many areas, but she was most famous throughout the territory for her skill as a midwife. Midwives were often the only medical practitioners around, male or female. The importance of children and families, along with the support of male church leadership, made them high-profile members of Mormon society.

And Patty Sessions was, so to speak, the mother of all Mormon midwives. During Utah's early years, Patty helped many of the state's women give birth, delivering about 250 babies in her first year in Utah alone and a lifelong total of 3,977. Her gnarled and calloused but powerful hands were the first things many babies felt in their new world. Her friendly face—with weathered skin, long nose, and broad forehead often topped by an old-fashioned bonnet—was the first thing they saw.

Like most midwives, she learned her trade mostly through observation and trial and error, but she also attended medical lectures whenever she could. She was a member and later president of the Council of Health, a group dedicated to educating health professionals. She also presided over the Mormon women's group dedicated to helping disadvantaged members of the community, which would later become the church-wide Relief Society. "Much good done in both societies over which I presided," she wrote in her diary. "The [women] were cloked [sic] the sick and poor were visitet [sic] and administered to and their wants relieved [sic]."

After David died in 1850, Patty, then in her mid-fifties, maintained her own home, alone—but not for long. In 1851 John Parry, a musician and the first conductor of the Mormon Tabernacle Choir, asked her to marry him. In her journal she wrote, in her usual pragmatic tone: "I feel to thank the Lord that I have some one to cut my wood for me."

John took a second wife, but by this time little could faze Patty. She didn't hold it against him—even though, as in her first marriage, she ended up taking on most of the household responsibilities. That included earning much of the family's income through her orchards and work as a midwife. She was one of the early investors in Zions Cooperative Mercantile Institution (ZCMI); by 1883 she owned $16,000 worth of shares in the store—an incredible amount of wealth for a woman with such modest beginnings.

Always looking for extra income, she took in boarders and did the cooking, cleaning, and bookkeeping that entailed. Her hands never stopped moving; she was constantly making gifts for people by hand or on her loom, even into very old age—though by then, she was nearly blind and the recipients often had to redo her work. Apparently, doing something poorly wasn't enough to stop her from doing it. She also frequently gave to charity, dutifully paying her church tithing and adding extra funds to help pay others' passage to Utah.

All the while Patty kept teaching and learning—including those dance lessons—well into very old age.

John Parry died in 1868, and Patty once again settled into running her own household and affairs. In 1870 she moved to Bountiful, a town her son helped found north of Salt Lake City. Building on a lifelong love of education, she used proceeds from the ZCMI mercantile to create the Patty Sessions Academy, housed in an attractive brick building, where all were welcome to send their children for a free education. Of course, she taught the classes. This was in 1883, when she was eighty-eight years old.

Patty continued tending the sick as well as her orchard into her nineties. A diary entry in 1886, when she was ninety-one, reads, "We have got the corn hauled here & stacked." When she was ninety-three, she recorded going for sleigh rides almost every day and clearing snow off her house after a storm. Patty Sessions wrote her last known diary entry in 1888. She died in 1892, when she was ninety-seven.

Patty Sessions's diaries are a detailed and invaluable record of life in the early days of the Church of Jesus Christ of Latter-day Saints. But they are also a look into the mind of a particularly strong-willed powerhouse. In her homespun language she expressed her feelings later in life: "I have been reading my journal and I feel to thank the Lord that I have passed through what I have," she wrote. "I have gained an experience I could not have gained no other way."

Eliza R. Snow

(1804–1887)

POET AND PRIESTESS

When a magazine in Utah printed an article theorizing about "Mortal and Immortal Elements of the Human Body," a matter of Mormon church doctrine, the story provoked a negative reaction from an important reader: Brigham Young, the president of the church. The article "places me under obligations to correct the minds of the Latter-day Saints," he wrote in a public response. "On some future occasion when I have time, I may possibly take up the article in detail, but at present shall simply say, as the Prophet Joseph Smith once told an Elder who asked his opinion of a so-called revelation he had written—'It has just one fault, and that one fault is, it is not true.'"

One might feel sorry for the man called out by the forbidding Young. But even though the writer was one of Young's closest confidantes, it wasn't a man. It was Eliza R. Snow, one of his wives and the most powerful woman in Utah.

Few trifled with Brigham Young. Eliza Snow was one of the few who could. In this instance she finally backed down to Young and acknowledged that he was right—six months later in a tiny newspaper notice.

Of all the figures who loom large in founding the Mormon church, few threw a bigger shadow than Eliza R. Snow. Martha Cannon, herself a force to be reckoned with, called Snow the church's "grandest woman." In fact, Eliza was sometimes called "Presidentess," which indicated her role as something akin to a female president of the church. Other titles included "captain of Utah's woman-host" and "Zion's poetess."

Her influence was both direct and implicit; she presided over some enterprises and was asked to give opinions, support, and advice on

Eliza R. Snow, Brigham Young's wife and close adviser, was known for both her impeccable appearance and her steely will.

pretty much everything else. Men and women admired her, and Brigham Young counted her as one of his closest advisers.

A childless woman, she reminded other women that their individual contributions to the church were as important as motherhood and that they could ensure they contributed best by becoming fully developed as people.

And she did her best to be an example of what she taught. Tall and graceful, with a delicate face and elegant bearing, she was known for her feminine beauty as well as her steely will.

She dressed impeccably in flowing gowns that accented her figure. One of Brigham Young's daughters described her as "slight and fragile and always immaculate in dress. I see her now in her full-skirted, lace-trimmed caps and a gold chain around her neck, looking for all the world like a piece of Dresden china."

Her deep-set eyes and penetrating gaze made people in her presence feel as if she could look into their very souls. But she was also witty and often very funny, with a dry humor that frequently came out in her writing. It's easy to see why people respected her and were even devoted to her.

Eliza Roxcy Snow was born in 1804 and grew up in Ohio, where she went to school and worked as a secretary for her father, a justice of the peace. An intelligent young woman and a quick learner, she started writing poetry while she was still a child and published poems in local magazines and newspapers.

Eliza met Joseph Smith in a nearby town in 1831, shortly after he founded the Church of Jesus Christ of Latter-day Saints. When she heard about what Mormons believed to be the restoration of the ancient gospel in modern times, the deeply religious Eliza found "what my soul hungered for," something she at first thought was "a hoax—too good to be true." She was convinced partly by Joseph Smith's sincerity when he visited her family. When the church moved its headquarters to Kirtland,

Ohio, in 1835, Eliza followed, working as a teacher. Rather than have her own house built, she lived with Joseph and his wife, Emma, and donated her inheritance to help build a temple.

From the beginning, Eliza was an integral part of the church hierarchy. She helped convert her beloved younger brother, Lorenzo, who would become the church's fifth president. She was also secretly "sealed" to Joseph Smith and after his death married his successor, Brigham Young—one of many women joined to them in "celestial" or spiritual marriage. She considered her marriage to Joseph Smith one of the most important events in her life and referred to him as her "first and only love."

Church members called Eliza a "priestess," and Joseph Smith chose her to officiate in the Nauvoo Temple as head of the women temple workers. (Men did the rites for other men, and women did them for women.) Important women in the early church were "set apart" to give blessings to the sick, something Eliza did often, sometimes with friends including midwife Patty Sessions.

On one visit Patty wrote that she "with ER Snow blessed Helen and Genette. Then in the gift of tongues ER Snow sung a blessing to all the rest of the girls." Eliza and other women also claimed to have the "gift of tongues" and found it an important part of their lives, though they were discouraged from doing it too much. They also held informal prayer circles.

As well as an organizer, Eliza was a writer, and she is still fondly regarded for her contributions to church literature and music. She eventually wrote or edited nine books, including two books of her poetry. Like her, her poems tended to be filled with a sense of passion and conviction, incorporating fiery or flowery language.

She was a sought-after public speaker known for an ability to put a rousing speech together on the fly. Through her impassioned writing, she instilled church teachings about various points of doctrine in church members' minds, an influence that continues even now. Today the official Mormon hymnbook includes ten of her songs.

In 1845, after her father's death, she wrote the hymn "O My Father" to express her ideas about meeting loved ones again in God's presence after death. Like her other hymns, it is still popular in the church today. It reveals Eliza's idea of a godly mother as well as a father in heaven:

> *In the heavens are parents single?*
> *No, the thought makes reason stare!*
> *Truth is reason, truth eternal*
> *Tells me I've a mother there.*

Eliza passionately believed in the importance of an afterlife. She saw the next phase of existence as a place where all people, men and women, would be equal, and all wrongs made right—at least for those who lived up to God's (and Eliza's) expectations:

> *When I leave this frail existence,*
> *When I lay this mortal by,*
> *Father, Mother, may I meet you*
> *In your royal courts on high?*
> *Then, at length, when I've completed*
> *All you sent me forth to do,*
> *With your mutual approbation*
> *Let me come and dwell with you*

These ideas would go on to have great influence over the way Mormon doctrine was taught to those who came after her.

Along with Patty Sessions, Eliza helped found the Relief Society, the charitable organization that today includes all Mormon women. It was originally a way for women to pool their energies to help the poor and the sick. When it was founded, the honor of heading the group went to Emma Smith, first wife of Joseph Smith and one of Eliza's friends. But Eliza Snow was its secretary and the powerhouse behind its development. In 1842 Eliza wrote a petition to the governor of Illinois, asking him to protect Joseph Smith. It was signed by hundreds of women, and she, along with Emma Smith, delivered it in person.

But their efforts to keep him safe would be in vain. Scuffles between Mormons and their neighbors boiled over into outright violence. When Joseph Smith was killed by an angry mob in 1844, Eliza was both grief-stricken and galvanized by the martyrdom of her prophet and husband. She was personally devoted to him, but she also saw him as a spiritual leader and a man infused with the spirit of God. As a secret wife, she had to do much of her mourning in private, but his death was a devastating blow.

Proud of her status as a granddaughter of Revolutionary War patriots, she felt betrayed as well as heartbroken when fellow Americans killed Joseph Smith and pushed the Mormons out of Illinois. She transferred her love for him and pain over his death into her work for the church, throwing herself into building it with a zeal that would never abate.

As the Saints set off for Utah, they faced bitter cold and rough territory without time to thoroughly prepare, and the trek was fraught with problems. Eliza consoled herself by writing, running the gamut from angry and emotional diary entries to songs encouraging the Saints on their way to the new home they would call "Zion." In a diary entry from February 1846, she wrote: "Snowstorm commenced in the night and continued thro' the day. It was so disagreeably cold that I did not leave the buggy. Suffered considerably from a severe cold. Amused myself by writing the following." She went on to write seven verses she called "The Camp of Israel: A Song for the Pioneers."

A few days later, she added five more verses, and even more a few weeks later:

> Let us go—let us go where our rights are secure—
> Where the waters are clear and the atmosphere pure—
> Where the hand of oppression has never been felt—
> Where the blood of our prophets has never been spilt.

She drove a team of oxen for much of the long trek across the plains, at night taking out her paper and pen and writing more poems and songs. Eliza's natural abilities to lead a group came to the forefront as she also gathered with other women for comfort, support, spiritual sustenance, and occasionally even fun.

After Joseph's death Emma Smith had stayed in Illinois while the Saints moved to Utah, and Brigham Young put the Relief Society on hold. In 1866 he and Eliza worked together to revive it.

With her counselors Zina D. H. Young and Elizabeth Ann Whitney, Eliza toured the new Mormon settlements Brigham Young was organizing all over the West. She was a treasured visitor for her Relief Society sisters, who saw her as their leader and revered her almost as much as they did the male church prophets. She would leave the "sisters" more enthusiastic about their faith and energized for the hardships that inevitably lay ahead. She encouraged women to hold regular meetings in each other's homes, organized so that half were dedicated to service projects and the other half to discussing church doctrine.

In 1880, when she was seventy-six, Eliza and her good friend, counselor, and fellow Brigham Young wife Zina took a train and a series of carriages along the rough roads to southern Utah. In one letter reporting on their five-month journey, Eliza wrote with her usual humor, "The morning was delightful, and the beautifully variegated mountain scenery, like a panorama constantly changing, was sublimely amusing as we passed on over rugged rocks and through [canyon] and dell, with ever and anon a healthy jolt, all of which were accredited for my especial benefit."

The visit wasn't all fun: She also met a young boy who was sick and beseeched her for help. A woman who witnessed the event wrote,

Sister Snow told the children to arise to their feet, close their eyes, and repeat after her the prayer, one sentence at a time. She prayed for the sick boy. When they got through praying he got up, walked home, and got into a wagon without help. He was well from that time.

She also traveled beyond America's borders. In 1872, with funds collected by her Relief Society sisters, she joined church officials including her brother Lorenzo on a grand tour that included Europe and Palestine. She later collected her and others' correspondence from the journey in a book.

Her letters portray a curious, vibrant, and determinedly cheerful woman who took every chance to see new things and meet new people. She thought London, for example, a "grand metropolis." But she couldn't help adding that when asked what she thought of the city, "I invariably replied that, were I to shape it to my liking, I should, in the first place, take it to pieces and straighten out its streets." Of course, the new surroundings also inspired her to write a few poems along the way.

Eliza set a high standard for every member of the church, especially women. Demanding and uncompromising, she called on them to be demure, modest, and hardworking. "Greatness is usefulness" was one of her favorite slogans.

She often said that while she had no power over men (though she sometimes wanted it), perhaps they would follow women's examples. This might seem contrary to the ideals of the suffrage movement going on nationwide, which argued for giving women the right to vote. But she and other women saw the two as going hand in hand: women should vote, they said, precisely because they naturally had better morals than men.

Eliza helped organize the Young Ladies' Retrenchment Association on directions from Brigham Young. The word "retrenchment" came from the idea that young women should, in Young's words, "retrench from extravagance in dress, in eating and even in speech." He wanted women to avoid "everything that is not good and beautiful, not to make yourselves unhappy, but to live so you may be truly happy in this life and in the life to come."

Eliza was a master at getting people to do what she wanted them to. Sometimes that meant asking male leaders for approval after she made a decision, rather than before. When another woman suggested the idea of forming a church-wide organization for children, Eliza told her to go ahead and do it—then went to get permission from the church's male leaders.

Eliza was instrumental in founding the *Woman's Exponent,* an influential magazine for Mormon women. She also managed a store, called the Women's Commission House, where women could sell their homemade goods.

Brigham Young was one of a very few people who dared tell her no—and even he didn't do that very often. They disagreed in public a couple of times. Though she always backed down, it was only after some wrangling.

Originally united by their shared admiration for Joseph Smith, Eliza and Brigham Young grew to be respectful friends as the years went on. She was literally his "right-hand" woman: She sat at his right side during dinners at the sprawling Lion House, his main residence in the middle of downtown Salt Lake City. Eliza lived there with some of Brigham Young's other wives and their children, and the church's most prominent women loved to gather in her room there.

From its founding, the Relief Society was run by women, and women were always its main beneficiaries. While the men ran the day-to-day operations of the church itself, the women were leaders in their own right, running their own meetings and electing their own officers. Mormon women saw their female leaders as "the head of the women in the world."

Since men had no interest in being involved with the Relief Society, it was a place where women's considerable leadership skills could thrive. Wielding her forceful personality and iron will, she turned her attention to nearly every aspect of women's lives, becoming a standard-bearer and setting the rules of conduct Mormon women would aspire to thereafter.

Eliza was a vocal defender of polygamy, disputing the notion that it was degrading. Mormon women, she said, had plenty of power both in their relationships and their society. Eliza Snow saw herself and her lieutenants as a great example of this. "Do you know of any place on the face of the earth where a woman has more liberty, and where she enjoys such high and glorious privilege as she does here as a Latter-day Saint?" she asked, then answered her question: "No!"

Later in her life, after Brigham Young's death in 1880, Eliza finally talked publicly about her marriage to Joseph Smith, even calling herself Eliza Snow Smith. Polygamy gave her a strong connection to the church's two most powerful men—a connection she couldn't have had without it.

Eliza R. Snow died at the Lion House in 1887 and was buried in Brigham Young's private cemetery. She was eighty-three. At the time of her death, the Relief Society had more than 22,000 members in about 400 branches around the world.

True to form, she had already organized every detail of her own funeral. It included a poem—fitting for a woman who would always be known for giving poetic voice to a generation of her people and describing their stories in song:

'Tis not the tribute of a sigh . . .
From sorrow's heaving bosom drawn,
Nor tears that flow from pity's eye,
To weep for me when I am gone . . .
In friendship's mem'ry let me live . . .
For friendship holds a secret cord,
That with the fibres of my heart,
Entwines so deep, so close; 'tis hard
For death's dissecting hand to part!
I feel the low responses roll,
Like the far echo of the night,
And whisper, softly through my soul,
"I would not be forgotten quite."

JANE MANNING JAMES

(ca. 1820–1908)

ADVOCATE FOR EQUALITY

On Christmas Day in 1884, Jane Elizabeth James walked through the winter cold, her dress neatly pressed and her hair carefully coiffed. She came to the house of John Taylor, president of the Mormon church and Utah's most important man, and knocked on the door. Her heart was burning with a request she could no longer suppress.

Taylor wasn't home, so a few days later Jane poured her thoughts into a letter instead. It began: "I called at your house last Thursday to have some conversation with you concerning my future salvation."

Jane was asking to be allowed to do "sealings," special ceremonies in the Mormon temple. It was a request she would make often—and one that would be routinely denied. Performing temple ceremonies was something she, as an adult church member in good standing, would have been given—if she hadn't been Black.

As she did in other requests, she tried to reason with the man she hoped would change the rules by appealing to the president's sense of fairness.

"Inasmuch as this is the fulness of times and through Abraham's seed all mankind may be blessed," she asked, "is there no blessing for me?"

His reply was negative, as they often would be. The Council of Twelve Apostles, the governing board of the church, issued this typical response after another request: "Aunt Jane was not satisfied with this, and as a mark of dissatisfaction she applied again after this for sealing blessings, but of course in vain."

It is sad now to think how often Jane made requests of her church, and how often they were in vain. But she kept trying. The fact that

Through faith, kindness, and persistence, Jane Manning James worked to overcome racial boundaries. When this photo was taken, her family was among the most prosperous in her neighborhood. Courtesy of the Church Archives, The Church of Jesus Christ of Latter-day Saints others saw her as less than equal wasn't enough to convince her that it was true.

Utah has never had a large African-American population, but Black people have lived in Utah since the first group of pioneers arrived in 1847. Their lives as an obvious minority give us a sense of how Mormons and other residents of Utah saw people of color.

Jane James was the first free Black woman to arrive in Utah. Her gender gave her life an added dimension and sometimes added hardship. Her stubborn faith and neighborly disposition helped her become a well-known figure in early Utah and a symbol of perseverance in the face of the steepest odds.

Jane Elizabeth Manning was born in about 1820 and grew up in Connecticut. She was never enslaved, but her father died when she was a child, and Jane went to work as domestic servant for a white family to help support her parents and siblings. She had little time for formal schooling and never learned to write, though she did learn to read. She dictated her many letters and other writings through friends.

By the 1840s Mormon missionaries were fanning out across the northeastern United States, even as the church's base was moving westward to found new communities. Jane was baptized around 1841 and convinced some of her relatives to join. She was an ardent follower and, like many early members, felt church membership was a spiritual calling. So when the call came to move to "Zion," she was ready to accept the hardship that would entail. As her biographer, Henry J. Wolfinger, writes: "In other religions, conversion might be the final stage of professing faith, but in nineteenth-century Mormonism it was but an initial step followed by the convert's departure from 'Babylon' to 'Zion,' where he might join the faithful in the work of establishing the kingdom of God on earth."

It would have been hard to prepare for what lay ahead: a journey of about 750 miles, most of it by foot, with a high likelihood of meeting people who weren't sympathetic to the idea of free Black people. Even many of her fellow converts were less than helpful, generally failing to offer assistance to her and her young son, Sylvester, along the way.

As they covered the miles to the Mormon settlement of Nauvoo, Illinois, Jane and her son, along with her mother, her siblings, and their spouses, walked until their shoes wore out and their feet cracked and "bled until you could see the whole print of our feet with blood on the ground," Jane later recalled in her autobiography. Along the way Jane also lost the trunk containing many of her things, including clothes, when a steamboat captain denied them passage—after taking their luggage onboard. Their journey was all the harder because they were often delayed by officials who required more proof of their free status.

When the family arrived in Nauvoo, they met with their prophet, Joseph Smith, who told them God would protect and bless them. Joseph and Emma Smith took Jane in as a friend and a housekeeper. Having lost her belongings, she had nothing to set up her own household. Jane treasured her close relationship with the Smiths and called Joseph "the finest man I ever saw on earth." She would later recall many instances where Joseph and Emma were kind to her and treated her as an equal, apparently even offering to legally adopt her. Years later she would work persistently to make her acceptance of that offer official.

While she was living in Nauvoo, Jane met and married Isaac James, a free Black man who had converted to Mormonism and had lived in Nauvoo since 1839.

The fact that Mormons baptized Black people and welcomed them into their community had helped inflame sentiment against them in the Mormons' first settlements in Missouri. Missouri was a slave-owning state, and some of its citizens suspected the Mormons would try to deprive them of their right to practice slavery.

In Nauvoo violence escalated again. In 1844 Joseph Smith, who was also mayor of Nauvoo, ran for president. He ran partly on a platform of ending legalized slavery, and his feelings on slavery were another reason for Jane's devotion to him. In 1844 Smith and other Nauvoo officials ordered town marshals to destroy an anti-Mormon newspaper, further inflaming sentiment against Mormons. When Smith declared martial law and assembled the town militia to protect Nauvoo, officials in surrounding towns accused him of treason against Illinois. Smith was killed by a mob while he awaited trial in nearby Carthage. The tensions between the Mormons and their neighbors mirrored tensions between people all over America who couldn't agree about a national policy on slave ownership.

Along with many others Jane decided to move west, to the other side of the Rocky Mountains, in hope of escaping persecution. In 1846, during the trek west, she gave birth to a son she named Silas. She was one of many women who had to pause on their journey to have a child, realizing they could rest only briefly before moving on again. She and Isaac were among the lead company heading across the plains, and they were among the first to arrive in the Salt Lake Valley in the summer of 1847. They walked much of the way, facing harsh weather, dust storms, and a lack of food for their livestock.

The Jameses weren't the only Black church members arriving in Utah. Some of the Black Saints were free; others were enslaved by church members. Although Joseph Smith and Brigham Young personally opposed the institution of slavery, they allowed their membership to keep the people they owned before they joined the church. Three Black men entered the Salt Lake Valley with the first Mormon wagon train in July of 1847. One of them was Green Flake, a servant of one of the pioneer families, who drove the wagon that carried church president Brigham Young into the valley.

Samuel D. Chambers, one of the church's first Black members, lived on the East Coast when he was baptized in 1844. At the time, he was enslaved, which meant he wasn't free to associate with fellow Mormons until twenty-one years later. After the Civil War he moved to Utah and was a successful farmer with his own land.

By 1870 there were about 120 Black people in Utah, about one-tenth of one percent of the population. Like their white counterparts, their faith galvanized them, even as they faced the same trials with the added difficulty of being considered second-class citizens in Utah as in the rest of America.

The Salt Lake Valley was arid, with weather that varied from below freezing in winter to more than one hundred degrees in summer. The pioneers had to build houses and set up farms and irrigation systems with no outside help. The James family, like many pioneers, suffered poverty and near starvation when crops failed. But even then Jane gave food to other desperate families. Eliza Lyman, the wife of a church official, wrote in 1849 that "Jane James, the colored woman, let me have two pounds of flour, it being half of what she had."

For the most part, white Saints didn't discriminate against Black people in a heavy-handed fashion. But that doesn't mean Mormons were free of prejudice. They believed Black people bore "the mark of Cain," that their color marked them as descendants of Cain, the Bible's original villain, who killed his brother in one of the Bible's first stories. Whites believed Black people couldn't be treated equally until God lifted the curse on them. This was similar to, and no doubt influenced by, the feelings of most white Americans at the time, who believed God favored them over people of color.

So, while Mormons didn't perpetrate acts of violence against Black people, they felt it was logical for Black people to hold an inferior place in society. Brigham Young favored indentured servitude, in which Black people worked as servants but were not "owned" by whites. "It is a great blessing to the seed of Adam to have the seed of Cain as servants," Young wrote. "But those they serve should use them with all the heart and feeling, as they would use their own children, and their compassion should reach over them and round about them, and treat them as kindly, and with that human feeling necessary to be shown to mortal beings of the human species."

But Young believed in the curse of Cain and felt that prevented Black people from holding the priesthood—a designation normally given to all adult male members who follow church precepts. "That curse will remain upon them, and they never can hold the Priesthood or share in it until all the other descendants of Adam have received the promises and enjoyed the blessings of the Priesthood and the keys thereof," he said. "Until the last ones of the residue of Adam's children are brought up to that favourable position, the children of Cain cannot receive the first ordinances of the Priesthood. They were the first that were cursed, and they will be the last from whom the curse will be removed."

Inequality was a part of church practice until 1978, when Black men were finally allowed to hold the priesthood and become full-fledged lay clergy (though at least one Black man, Elijah Abel, was actually given the priesthood during Joseph Smith's lifetime, demonstrating that the denial wasn't a hard rule until later). Black church members knew they would probably not be treated equally with whites in Utah—but they also knew they wouldn't be treated equally anywhere else in America, either.

Isaac James worked for Brigham Young, and, like most of their neighbors, the family also ran a farm and owned their own plot of land close to downtown Salt Lake City. The couple had six additional children, five of whom survived to adulthood. They lived near and were friends with the handful of fellow African Americans in the area, but they also socialized with white people. Whatever their ideas about Black people, anyone who met Jane came away thinking of her as a dignified woman who took great care in the way she dressed and carried herself.

The Jameses were subsistence farmers at first but gradually scraped enough money together to buy sheep and horses. They eventually rose to be one of the most prosperous families in their neighborhood—quite a feat considering their lack of formal education and resources.

But that doesn't mean things were easy, and they weren't going to get any easier. In 1869 Isaac left the family, taking some property with him and selling the rest to his wife. Jane was left to fend for herself.

It's hard to say why their marriage didn't work out. Perhaps all the household responsibilities weighed on Isaac too heavily. Maybe his faith in the church was wavering. Whatever the reason, he left not just Jane but Utah, and she didn't hear from him for years. He returned to Salt Lake City from Portland, Oregon, shortly before his death in 1890.

Jane remarried four years after Isaac left, but that marriage only lasted two years before it ended in divorce. Her unlucky love life was reflected in her autobiography, which didn't even mention her divorce or second marriage. She did ask to be "re-sealed" to Isaac after he returned—a request that reflected the ceremony's importance.

By this time Jane's children were mostly grown. But she did have to care for younger children at home, and her husband's income had disappeared along with him. She moved to a smaller house, near what is now Liberty Park, and worked as a domestic servant, cleaning and washing clothes, work she knew all too well. She probably had little choice in the matter, since white-collar jobs weren't open to Black women at the time no matter how resourceful, hardworking, or faithful they were. She would never again attain the financial security she had at the height of her prosperity.

Throughout the years, Jane supported her children financially, giving them money and property when they grew up. As was common in those times, her family faced the hardships of disease and poor medical care as well as poverty. Five of her seven children died before their fortieth birthdays; two of those were daughters who died in childbirth. But her eldest son, Sylvester, was listed in 1869 as a member of the Nauvoo Legion of Mormon soldiers and would go on to become a successful landowner himself.

Aside from her children and grandchildren, the most important thing in Jane's life was her church, and she worked tirelessly throughout her life to contribute. She was active in charitable work through the church's Relief Society. In return, the women of the society, undoubtedly aware that she was giving despite her own limited means, sometimes gave her holiday food baskets. One symbol of her status in the church: She also had a place of honor reserved for her in one of the front pews in the Salt Lake Tabernacle, site of the church's most important public meetings.

Even as she worked and sacrificed on behalf of the church, Jane was frustrated by the ways the church treated her differently because of her race. Over and over, she made requests of church leaders. More than anything, she wanted to be able to do temple ceremonies on behalf of herself and her relatives, a privilege granted only to members in good standing—and usually only to white members.

This was no small matter: Mormons believed they needed these ceremonies to make it into heaven. So not only was it painful for Jane to not have access to all of them, she believed it was dangerous to her very soul. It must have been painful to know that not all the blessings the church offered were open to her.

She didn't accept this quietly. Instead, she dictated letter after letter, reminding the authorities that she, too, was human, and that Joseph Smith had told her she deserved the blessings of heaven. Though the leaders told her she had to be patient and wait for word from God allowing Black members to have all the rights whites had, she was tired of waiting.

Jane also knew about Black members like Elijah Abel, who had been given all the benefits open to white members before officials clamped down in the intervening decades (the priesthood wasn't formally denied to Black members until 1847). He, too, petitioned for permission to be allowed in the temple after a lifetime of service to the church. And like Jane, though many of his requests were denied, he remained a faithful member throughout his life, even going to Canada to preach as a missionary shortly before his death in 1884.

Jane and Elijah believed, as all Mormons did, that the restoration of the "true church" meant humanity had entered the "latter days," which meant God would once again reveal new commandments and blessings to his faithful. Had church members not been promised that the latter days meant forgiveness for the sins of Cain?

Her requests were sometimes granted, partly because she knew many church leaders personally, partly because they knew about her church and charitable work, and partly because she never gave up. When someone said no, Jane politely kept asking, quietly breaking down barriers along the way.

It took many requests and a lot of persistence for Jane to get permission to work in the temple—a huge victory for her. Even when she did get that permission, a white woman stood in for her in the actual temple ceremonies. It was even harder to gain official recognition as a member of Joseph Smith's family. When it was finally offered, it was not as a daughter. It was as an eternal servant—the way outsiders had seen her all her life. Her repeated pleas are a heartbreaking symbol of the inequality she faced less because she was a woman than because of her race.

An influx of Black newcomers—many of them not Mormon— moved into Utah in the 1880s and 1890s, mostly for railroad, mining, and military jobs in the "Crossroads of the West." By the time Jane reached old age, the number of fellow African Americans in Utah had grown significantly, though it was still a small part of the population. Utah was less restrictive when it came to civil rights than many other states, which at the time were increasingly institutionalizing segregation. Jane's son Sylvester, for example, was well-known and respected even after his mother's death.

Jane James died in 1908, with some of her hopes fulfilled and others still waiting. Before she died, she dictated her autobiography, just as she had dictated all those letters to church leaders. "I want to say right here that my faith in the gospel of Jesus Christ of Latter-day Saints is as strong today—nay, it is if possible stronger—than it was the day I was first baptized," it says. "I pay my tithes and offerings, keep the Word of Wisdom. I go to bed early and arise early. I try in my feeble way to set a good example to all."

Despite her trials, her faith in the church never wavered, and she remained convinced that someday church leaders would accept Black members as full participants in it. Black church members during her time and ever since have looked to her as a symbol of the power of faith and a pioneer in both the church and Black members' role within it. Modern-day admirers have brought her to life for a new generation through novels, a stage play, and a handful of films. In 2005 a group of church members placed a memorial plaque in the Salt Lake Cemetery dedicated to her memory. A monument to Black Utah pioneers at This Is the Place Heritage Park, dedicated in 2022, includes a statue of her.

A crowd of those who knew her attended her funeral, including some of the church's highest officeholders. Church president Joseph Fielding Smith was one of the speakers. The *Deseret News* reported, "The house was crowded, many in the congregation being of her own race. Flowers in profusion were contributed by friends who had learned to respect the deceased for her undaunted faith and goodness of heart." This persistent yet kindhearted woman had, despite prejudices and disadvantages, become one of her community's most beloved figures.

EMMELINE B. WELLS

(1828–1921)

JOURNALIST AND ACTIVIST

As she rode the train to Washington, Emmeline Wells was nervous. Perched like a small, sprightly bird next to her traveling companion, Zina Young Williams, she had a speech to refine—a difficult job, even though by now she was used to preparing speeches. She just hoped she could represent her cause well. As she always did for such occasions, she wore her best blue dress and trademark scarf, an outfit both beautiful and dignified.

Emmeline was always a little nervous speaking in front of a crowd, even when they were people she knew. But she had never talked to a crowd like this: The 1879 National Woman Suffrage Association meeting would draw women from around the country and receive media attention everywhere. And after that speech she was on her way to talk to members of the U.S. Congress.

Things were about to get even trickier: Even as she rode the train on her way to the national convention in Washington, D.C., the U.S. Supreme Court was declaring polygamy unconstitutional. Thus, she would have to defend an illegal practice on a national stage at a time when most Americans were appalled by it—just after it failed its last attempt to gain any legitimacy.

It was a daunting assignment. But Emmeline, the editor of a prominent women's magazine in Utah, had plenty of practice winning over an audience.

Emmeline Wells was one of the great communicators of her day. As a journalist and a leading proponent of a woman's right to vote, she spent thirty years traveling, speaking to the U.S. Congress and president, and representing Utah in national women's groups.

This photo of Emmeline B. Wells, editor of the Woman's Exponent magazine, was taken at about the time she spoke at the 1879 National Woman Suffrage Association meeting in Washington, D.C.

On that 1879 trip she did speak at the convention and to Congress. She even met Lucy Hayes, the nation's first lady, who encouraged Emmeline in her efforts to win women the vote and work toward making Utah a strong national voice on issues important to women and children.

Though she and her fellow Mormon women never did win complete sympathy for her church in the rest of the country, Emmeline did gain many admirers. An 1890 article in the *Century* magazine, a popular national publication, described Wells as "a woman of education and refinement; a finely organized person, with the emotional and religious traits largely developed. For forty years she has been an earnest and devout Mormon woman—wife and mother. There are thousands like her in earnestness and devotion to the faith, though few, perhaps, who are her equals intellectually."

Emmeline Wells was born in Massachusetts on leap year day, February 29, 1828, and joined the Mormon church at age fourteen. Educated at a prestigious New England school, she went to work as a teacher before moving to Nauvoo, Illinois, in 1844 with her new husband and his parents. She later recalled meeting Joseph Smith: "When he took my hand, I was simply electrified—thrilled through and through to the tips of my fingers, and every part of my body, as if some magic elixir had given me new life and vitality . . . the one thought that stilled my soul was, I have seen the Prophet of God, he has taken me by the hand."

The next two decades were difficult. Her marriage was short-lived; her first child, a son, died as an infant, and her husband abandoned her. She then married Newel Whitney, a prominent church member with whom she traveled to Utah in 1848. He died in 1850, leaving her to care for their two daughters. In 1852 she married Daniel H. Wells and had three more daughters, two of whom died young.

Daniel Wells, a second counselor to Brigham Young in the church presidency, already had six other wives. Emmeline didn't live with the rest of the family. The arrangement often left her lonely, though she loved her house on State Street in downtown Salt Lake City, which she also used as her office. She sometimes wistfully wrote of her dashed hopes for a close marital relationship and mourned, "He doesn't need me at all." Having survived two short marriages and now this, she seemed destined to find satisfaction only outside her personal life.

All these experiences, while trying, helped her develop the strength and independence that would propel her later on. Some successful people seem born powerful, but she didn't see herself as a naturally strong person. A tiny woman who stood a mere five feet tall, she was physically frail and often ill, and in private she tended to fret about her own fears and shortcomings. The main exception was writing, about which she once said, "I love this kind of work."

She credited her friends, family, and faith for her strength and a sense of humility that balanced out a sharp and sometimes sarcastic wit—characteristics that made others love her.

Emmeline did much of her work on the public stage when Utah was still a territory. The pioneers began wanting statehood soon after they arrived in 1847, but to many outside Utah, the idea was unthinkable. Congress was reluctant to grant statehood out of fear that Mormons would show more allegiance to their church leaders than to the U.S. government.

Tied in with the desire for statehood was that of many women to gain the right to vote. That was why Emmeline traveled to Washington to represent Utah at the national suffrage meeting.

Emmeline, known fondly by her readers as "Aunt Em," didn't begin her public life until after she had raised her daughters. She was forty-nine when she took up one of her favorite and most influential roles, as longtime editor of the *Woman's Exponent* newspaper. Emmeline took the post in 1877 (five years after the paper was founded by Louisa Greene) and held it for the next thirty-seven years. She was already leading a far-reaching effort by the Relief Society to harvest and store grain—such a success that the church had enough to sell its surplus to the U.S. government during World War I.

The twice-monthly *Exponent* was the first successful publication for women west of the Mississippi. Emmeline usually edited it in her small home office, poring over the details of which stories to print and how they should be written. From its inception, it was designed as a vehicle for women's concerns, as an early editorial explains: "We have no rivalry with any, no war to wage, no contest to provoke; yet we will endeavor, at all times, to speak freely on every topic of current interest, and on every subject as it arises in which the women of Utah, and the great sisterhood the world over, are specially interested."

The magazine was the unofficial voice of the Relief Society and the place where Mormon women could have their say on matters of society and politics as well as religion, and some of the state's most prominent women were contributors. It included everything from recipes and household tips to poetry to notices of upcoming events. It was a valuable way for women like Emmeline to communicate with— and gain support from—thousands of women at a time. These days, it serves as a record of what was important during its time. (She realized this, commenting that the *Exponent* would "furnish good material for future historians.")

Women's rights pioneer Susan B. Anthony recalled later in her book *History of Woman Suffrage:* "It is impossible to estimate the advantage this little paper gave to the women of this far western Territory. From its first issue it was the champion of the suffrage cause, and by exchanging with women's papers of the United States and England it brought news of women in all parts of the world to those of Utah."

By the 1870s Utah's population was rapidly expanding, buoyed by a constant influx of immigrants—both Mormon and not. A stream of people moving westward through Utah needed supplies. In 1869 the transcontinental railroad linked the eastern and western halves of the United

States and made travel through Utah easier and more common. The railroad, mining, and other industries brought more workers and wealth into the state, making Utah increasingly prosperous and sophisticated.

At the same time, a nationwide movement was gaining force: American women's quest for the right to vote. That desire was strong in Utah, where women had been voting in municipal elections since 1870. While others thought polygamy was barbaric and degrading, Mormon women said it gave them more freedom and responsibility than traditional marriage would have. And with the increasing strength of the Relief Society, women found many chances to exercise their leadership, business, and public speaking skills.

In its early years the Relief Society's structure and purpose were similar to those of the many other women's civic and religious societies springing up across the country. It brought women of various backgrounds together, blurring lines that would otherwise have divided them.

Some Mormon women were reluctant to take leadership roles. But in general, male and female church leaders encouraged women to take an active part in church life. Their roles brought them friendship, social bonds, ways to help each other, and a built-in avenue to consolidate their efforts toward any cause.

Church president Brigham Young supported their work. His words on the matter could have come from any number of national women's-rights advocates: "We believe that women are useful, not only to sweep houses, wash dishes, make beds, and raise babies, but that they should stand behind the counter, study law or physic [medicine], or become good bookkeepers and be able to do the business in any counting house, all this to enlarge their sphere of usefulness for the benefit of society at large."

Given all this, it's only natural that Mormon women would enter the world of politics, including the suffrage movement. But the women fighting for the vote back east weren't sure what to make of their Mormon counterparts. Some rallied in opposition to Utah women's suffrage on the grounds that it would make Mormons too influential on the national stage.

Emmeline served as a liaison between Mormon and non-Mormon women. Her admirers like to quote one of her most famous sayings: "I believe in women, especially thinking women." And Emmeline was a thinking woman. Representing Utah in the national fight for women's voting rights, she was a friend and colleague of such famous figures as Elizabeth Cady Stanton and Susan B. Anthony, who headed the National Woman Suffrage Association. Anthony was such a strong supporter that after one of Emmeline's speeches, she dashed up onto the stage to give Emmeline a hug.

National anti-polygamy legislation took away Utah women's voting rights in 1887. In 1889 Emmeline founded the Woman Suffrage Association of Utah, helping to make women's suffrage a condition of Utah's bid for statehood. She attended and spoke at a string of national conventions. When she was invited to conduct a plenary session at the 1893 World's Columbian Exposition in Chicago, she wrote with pride that it was the first time such an honor went to a Mormon woman. "If one of our brethren had such a distinguished honor conferred upon them, it would have been heralded the country over and thought a great achievement," she noted with trademark dry wit.

On her most ambitious trek, she traveled to the Woman's International Council and Congress in London in 1899. She also met with U.S. senators to answer their questions about Mormonism.

Emmeline was a sought-after speaker, known for her eloquence. In one of her speeches, she described her life and work:

> *I am not afraid of men, not the least in the world. I have often been on committees with men. I don't think it has hurt me at all, and I have learned a great deal. They have always been very good*

to me. We must stand up for the men. We could not do without
them. Certainly we could not have settled Utah without them.
They built the bridges and killed the bears; but I think the women
worked just as hard, in their way.

Despite all their efforts, and despite the admiration individual Mormon women gained in the eyes of their "gentile" counterparts, their battle for statehood—and with it, for their reinstated right to vote—would not become reality until the church publicly disavowed polygamy in 1890. The women involved in fighting on behalf of polygamy, many of whom had personal reservations about the practice, were all too happy to put that fight behind them and join everyone else in celebrating the territory's acceptance as a state in 1896.

She may have gotten a late start in being a leader, but growing older was no impediment for Emmeline. She published a popular book of poetry in 1896, the same year the Republican Party nominated her to run for the state senate (she lost to another woman, Martha Hughes Cannon). In 1912 she was the first woman to receive an honorary Doctor of Literature degree from Brigham Young University.

She was called to be church-wide president of the Relief Society in 1910, leaving the post shortly before her death in 1921. It was a demanding role, especially since by then she was eighty-two years old. She had already been the society's secretary for years, and she leaped into the job with the same dedication she gave everything else, instituting new programs and formalizing others, helping make the society into something close to what it is today—a worldwide institution that focuses Mormon women's charitable and religious efforts.

Her later life was not always a rosy success. The *Exponent,* which had struggled financially while she was editor, died after she left the publication, despite her attempts to save it by asking the Relief Society board to make it an official church-sponsored publication. In her final column she wrote that "to lay aside the editorial pen, even after so many long years, seems a hard task, but though the pen may be idle, the mind will ever gratefully remember all the associations which this little paper has been instrumental in creating."

In 1921, she was "released" from her post as the Relief Society president, a post that before then was a lifelong appointment (then again, she was in her nineties by this time and had served in the post for ten years).

When she died, businesses and institutions in Salt Lake City—including the newspaper the *Deseret News*—flew their flags at half-staff. After her death a bust of her was placed in the Utah State Capitol with the inscription "A Fine Soul Who Served Us." Emmeline would no doubt approve of that simple yet apt inscription.

CORNELIA PADDOCK

(1840–1898)
AUTHOR AND CRUSADER

In Cornelia Paddock's novel *In the Toils,* a woman decides she must leave Utah to spare her young daughter from being forced to marry a Mormon man "who had half a score of wives already." The woman's husband is a faithful Mormon, and he will bend to the will of church leaders. She must strike out alone. Leaving is dangerous, especially if the church sends its henchmen.

As the story goes, "The only hope left to the wife and mother was that of escaping by flight, and this hope hung on a very slender thread. Many had made the attempt and met their fate at the hands of the Destroying Angels before reaching the borders of the Territory. Others had been followed two and three hundred miles outside of the Territory and finally overtaken and killed, but a few had succeeded, and their success encouraged her to believe that escape was possible."

The church wasn't actually sending death squads out to kill women fleeing Utah. But Cornelia was willing to stretch the truth to aid a higher purpose—or to get more readers, depending on whom you ask.

As the battle over polygamy raged, the world outside Utah was eager to hear just how awful Mormon polygamists could be, and Cornelia Paddock was ready to tell them—in vivid novels that were read around the country.

Cornelia claimed her tales were based on stories told to her by Mormon women. Not only that, according to her, some of their revelations were so horrifying they were unfit for publication.

"Multitudes of facts that have come under my own observation during my long residence among this people, I dare not commit to paper. I

This image of Cornelia Paddock appeared in an 1887 reprint of the book Women of Mormonism, *edited by Jennie Froiseth. Cornelia wrote or contributed to several negative books about polygamy, including this one.* Reprinted from Women of Mormonism: The Story of Polygamy as Told by the Victims Themselves by Jennie Froiseth, 1887 (first published in 1882). (p.112)

have listened with feelings of sickening horror to the recitals of those who have suffered most from the workings of this abominable system miscalled religion, but I cannot give their story to the world," she wrote in the preface to *In the Toils*. "The characters of the story told in this book are real, the incidents are true, but I have told only a small part of the truth."

Cornelia Hill was born in New York in 1840. As an adult, she moved to Nebraska and married Alonzo G. Paddock, a miner who had worked in Utah off and on for years. The couple moved to Utah permanently in 1870 and would raise their four children in Salt Lake City. They were part of a wave of new residents arriving for economic reasons, not to be part of the Mormon kingdom.

Utah was becoming a hotbed of activities that had little to do with faith. Soldiers, sent by the federal government to keep an eye on the Mormons and Native Americans, prospected in their spare time. Some of them struck ore, leading to a mining boom that still hasn't ended. The transcontinental railroad linked East and West together, and feeder lines linked northern and southern Utah with the rest of the country. Suddenly, a lot of people wanted a piece of the economic pie Utah offered.

The Paddocks were among them. Alonzo Paddock held a few different clerical and mining-related jobs, none of which made much money. Cornelia was frustrated that it was so hard for "gentiles" to make a good living in Utah, since Mormons controlled much of the state's business and politics.

The increase in Utah's non-Mormon population made clashes inevitable. Mormon leaders preached self-sufficiency and looked inside their church for friends and business relationships. Americans feared that once Utah residents gained statehood and could vote in a national election, they would take orders from church headquarters.

For their part, the Mormons resented the influx of newcomers, which threatened to disrupt their carefully constructed community.

They felt the outsiders brought in unsavory elements and bad influences. They kept to themselves and tried not to draw negative attention, but outsiders felt threatened by their political and economic power and mystified by unusual elements of the religion.

Chief among those, of course, was polygamy. The uproar over it began almost immediately after word got out and only grew after the Mormons traveled to Utah. It was an easy target and a lightning rod for larger issues.

Cornelia Paddock was one of a few people who gained nationwide and even international fame by "exposing" Mormon practices to the world. A Methodist, she was appalled by polygamy and the ways she felt it demeaned women. Protestants were preaching in Utah as early as 1862, when the U.S. military established Fort Douglas in the foothills overlooking Salt Lake City under the command of General Patrick Connor. Connor made sure the fort always had a Protestant chaplain. Even as Utah Mormons sent missionaries out of the state, other religious groups were sending missionaries to preach throughout the West, including Utah.

While others used political avenues to end polygamy, Cornelia did it through writing. She was a prolific writer, focusing on home and family. Some of her sayings, such as "A mother's love perceives no impossibilities," still appear on greeting cards.

Cornelia is best known, though, for two novels in which Mormon men were the villains. She hoped crafting harrowing fiction based on the dark side of polygamy would gain her a wider and more receptive audience. "I have put my books on Mormonism into narrative form because I knew they would be more generally read if offered to the public in the guise of a story," she wrote.

She said her novels were based on true stories she had heard from women who had experienced polygamy. Some of her friends and colleagues were former Mormon wives, including Sarah M. Pratt, who divorced well-known church official Orson Pratt when he took another wife. Cornelia fictionalized the stories, she said, to preserve their subjects' privacy.

In her first book—*In the Toils; Or, Martyrs of the Latter Days*, published in 1879—a woman escapes from bloodthirsty Mormons who want to force her and her daughter into polygamy. The hero who frees them is General Patrick Connor himself. A strident opponent of polygamy in real life, he once called the Mormons in Utah "a community of traitors, murderers, fanatics, and whores."

Cornelia's second and most popular novel, *The Fate of Madame La Tour: A Tale of Great Salt Lake,* was published in 1881 and went on to sell more than 100,000 copies. In it Mormon men murder a wealthy woman's husband, take her money, and kidnap her daughter. Both novels begin with the westward migration from Missouri and depict its hardships, portraying that trek as the first step toward isolating converts from the rest of the country.

In Cornelia's books women are forced into polygamy through threats to themselves or their families if they don't obey. Other women in her books go along with it because they love their husbands and are afraid the men will leave them if they don't submit. She included an appendix of notes on the specific cases she said were the basis for the episodes in the novels.

However inflammatory her language and subject matter, it was widely agreed that Cornelia Paddock was a pretty good writer, telling her stories through fast-paced, absorbing narratives and active language. Her books got high marks from the national press. "We only wish every cultivated woman in the nation could read it," the Chicago *Inter-Ocean* enthused about *The Fate of Madame La Tour,* while the *Boston Gazette* called it "a vivid and startling picture of the people and the manners with which it deals."

Cornelia wrote her books at a time when national interest in polygamy and the Mormon church were at their peak; she and her publishers capitalized on her firsthand knowledge of life in Utah and the intense public arguments over polygamy.

People around the country felt they knew Cornelia and turned to her as an expert on Utah and Mormons. Her authority was bolstered by support from many prominent "gentiles," including authorities appointed to oversee Utah by the federal government and politicians elected by an increasingly diverse population. Several of them even wrote prefaces to her book. Utah Territory governor Eli H. Murray wrote, "Her writings attest her capacity, which, joined with her long residence in Utah and access to reliable sources of information, suggest a true story well told." A state supreme court justice added another recommendation.

Cornelia wasn't worried as much about Mormon political power as she was about the "degrading" effect polygamy had on women. She saw it as something akin to slavery (as did some other activists). She thought no woman in her right mind would choose such a lifestyle, and no good man would force her into it. Therefore, women were being seduced, forced, or brainwashed, while men were exercising too much power or, even worse, catering to their baser desires.

Cornelia felt she, and all "good Christian women," had a moral obligation to help Mormon women break the bonds of polygamy. "The man who cannot keep one family in comfort certainly cannot keep three or four," Cornelia wrote, adding that she had heard the men most interested in polygamy were "drunken, brutal wretches who, as a friend of mine once said, 'cannot be content with making one woman miserable for life.'"

Cornelia's Mormon neighbors told her to mind her own business, but she wouldn't back down. "It is my business because I am a woman, and polygamy degrades my sex below the level of humanity; because I am a wife, and polygamy makes that sacred name a by word; because I am a mother, and polygamy makes maternity a curse, and puts the brand of shame on the innocent foreheads of little children," she wrote.

She was hardly alone in her views. All across America women were speaking out against social ills, forming "temperance unions" to battle alcohol consumption and working to save "fallen" women including prostitutes and teenage girls whom they saw as targets of lascivious men. They believed women were clearly morally superior to men, which is one reason they wanted women to be able to vote (some of the women fighting polygamy came from the ranks of those fighting for women's suffrage—though others in the movement were friendly with Utah's Mormon suffrage activists). In every way, they felt, women should spread and enforce good behavior.

Cornelia was one of a handful of writers using Mormon practices as fodder for their stories. Just as it was fashionable to write about women being kidnapped by Native Americans, Mormons were a common target, either as primary or secondary characters, in the highly dramatic style popular at the time. Decades later, some of those same themes would be made into movies.

The author's novels weren't her only vehicle in the fight. In 1878 a handful of concerned women in Salt Lake City launched the Ladies Anti-Polygamy Society, with Cornelia as its secretary. They sent petitions to politicians, asking for stronger enforcement of anti-polygamy laws, and submitted letters and articles to newspapers and magazines. Cornelia's writing skills made her one of the group's most active spokespeople. She was a regular contributor to the *Salt Lake Tribune,* a daily newspaper that at the time was strongly opposed to many of the church's social, political, or philosophical policies and influences.

Cornelia also contributed to compilations of writing about Mormons. One, called *Hand-book on Mormonism,* was published in 1882. It professed to be an objective overview of Mormon belief and life for a national audience, going into detail about theology, temple work, and the organization of the church. It exaggerated some things and seems to have made others up, like the assertion that Mormons used more profanity than other people.

Cornelia's contribution was entitled "Are Mormon Women Happy in Polygamy?" In answer to the question, she related stories from Mormon women who were forced into polygamy. One woman, Cornelia said, fainted three times on her way home from the temple where Brigham Young commanded that she give permission for her husband to take another wife. Another one said, "The plains, from the Missouri to this valley, are strewed with the bones of those whom this system has killed, and the cemetery on the hill is full of them, but every one of those women is now wearing a martyr's crown."

An ad in the back of the book described the forthcoming *Women of Mormonism,* which the publisher promised would be "The Most Thrilling Book of the Age!" Cornelia was also a contributor to that book. Edited by Jennie Froiseth, it compared Mormon polygamy to other "barbarian" practices, including Middle Eastern harems. Jennie toured the country with Cornelia, lecturing about the evils of polygamy. Clearly, the salacious nature of polygamy stories was one of the things that captured the public's attention—and publishers had no qualms about capitalizing on that.

It's hard to reconcile Cornelia's view with those of Mormon women such as Martha Cannon and Eliza R. Snow, who said they went into polygamy willingly—and that the lifestyle even had its benefits. Both sides exaggerated their points to capture an audience and win support. With such powerful rhetoric flying, there was no love lost between women fighting for and against polygamy.

In 1880 Cornelia's group formed the Women's National Anti-Polygamy Society, hoping to get national support, and started publishing its own newspaper, the *Anti-Polygamy Standard.* Cornelia was one of the main contributors, making the case that polygamy was not only degrading but also not Christian.

Echoing anti-polygamy activists on the national level, she said polygamy was like slavery and Mormon men were no better than slave owners. In fact, she argued, these men were worse, because they were keeping women hostages to fulfill their base sexual desires. They hoped this suggestion, coming fifteen years after the Civil War, would convince readers that polygamy required action. How could the country fight a war over the rights of enslaved people, only to leave these women in bondage?

Even though Mormon women defended polygamy and railed against her writings, Cornelia refused to call them her opponents. Instead, she expressed sympathy for them, saying they had no choice in their situation and needed help to get out. This didn't go over well with the Mormon women, who fought back through their own publication, the *Woman's Exponent,* saying Cornelia and her colleagues didn't know what they were talking about. Both sides claimed to have moral high ground, saying they were only doing God's will in making a stand on their side of the battle.

By the early 1880s Cornelia and her fellow activists were starting to see some success. In 1884 they gathered 250,000 signatures for a petition asking Congress to end polygamy. Partly based on stories they heard from Cornelia and other writers, Congress passed legislation specifying penalties for anyone caught practicing polygamy.

The activists were frustrated by the many women who refused to leave polygamy. A group that included Cornelia and Angie Newman, a Methodist missionary from Vermont, decided the problem was that fleeing Mormon women had no place to go. In Cornelia's mind, that made them little different from heathen anywhere else in the world who needed material support as well as salvation.

The Methodists' response was to form the Industrial Christian Home Association of Utah and set up a place where refugees from Mormon marriages could live, get an education, and start making money for themselves. Those tools would help the women to feel safe in leaving the church and eventually live in regular society. Once Mormon women knew they could escape to this shelter, the activists believed, they would leave in droves.

The Industrial Home was similar to partnerships set up elsewhere to help "fallen women"—that is, prostitutes—inviting comparisons that didn't win the activists any friends among the Mormons. At the same time, Cornelia herself was criticized as a hypocrite when her fourteen-year-old son, who had already committed a few minor crimes, was the ringleader in a sexual assault on a teenage boy. Cornelia argued that her son was "mentally incompetent," but he served some jail time for an event that led to both anguish and embarrassment for a woman who hoped to tell other women how to be good wives and mothers.

Harsh words flew thick and fast, with opponents on both sides claiming to be the more virtuous and God-fearing while flinging insults at the other side. The comparisons to prostitution essentially portrayed polygamy supporters as madams who led innocent young women into lives of sexual servitude (the *Salt Lake Tribune* called Mormon men "male prostitutes"). Mormons fired back that the real fallen women were the ones signing petitions against them, occasionally accusing them of being whores. The *Exponent* called the activists' allegations a "filthy abuse of the people of this territory."

The Christian home was a popular idea among polygamy opponents, but it didn't attract as many women as the activists had hoped, partly because Mormon women didn't respond well to the notion that their religion was immoral and the Protestant missionaries' brand of Christianity was better. Although some Mormons continued to practice polygamy for decades, the fight over it largely ended with the 1890 "Woodruff Manifesto," a public declaration that the Mormon church would no longer support the practice. The Industrial Christian Home Association of Utah closed in 1892, much to Mormons' glee.

But Cornelia hadn't given up on the idea of helping unfortunate women. In 1894 she opened the Woman's Home Association, dedicated to helping prostitutes find housing and legitimate means of employment. It was a difficult project. While the home for Mormon refugees got

$40,000 in government funding, helping fallen women wasn't as popular. She had a hard time finding anyone who would rent space to her, leading her to remark on the irony that "there have always been some property owners willing to rent houses to those who do not wish to reform"—that is, prostitutes.

Without much support, and having little money of her own, Cornelia couldn't make the home work. She focused instead on finding work for women who might otherwise be forced into prostitution to make a living. She found them domestic jobs or employed them directly as seamstresses in a sewing room she ran in her Salt Lake City offices.

Cornelia spent much of her time either asking for donations or trying to convince women to take advantage of her offer. Funding was always sporadic, and donations were generally small. Cornelia bemoaned the fact that she didn't have enough money to help all the women who needed it. She eventually was forced to close her sewing room, though she continued to work at helping down-on-their-luck women until her death in 1898.

Cornelia's writing and activism added fuel to the fire that eventually forced the end of Mormon polygamy. Her eye-popping tales helped sway national opinion and galvanize politicians to act.

While some saw Cornelia as a publicity hound—using salacious stories to further her career and fame—her work to help outcast women, despite her own financial hardships, says otherwise. Like the Mormons she battled, she thought she was doing God's work. Like many of them, she spent her life doing what she thought might make the world a better place for women.

ANN ELIZA WEBB YOUNG

(1844-?)

WIFE NO. 19

B righam Young was a powerful man and a ferocious enemy. The leader of the Mormon church during the early years of Utah settlement, he might be best known for his many wives. Some of those women loved the prominence their status as a wife of the prophet gave them, and some of his wives (including Eliza R. Snow) were among the most powerful and respected people in Utah.

But not all of his wives were happy, and one woman's discontent brought her national fame. Even now, more than one hundred years later, Ann Eliza Webb is one of the best known of Brigham Young's wives— but not for positive reasons. She loathed the time she spent as his wife, and when she suffered, she didn't do it in silence. She wrote a tell-all book, *Wife No. 19,* about her marriage to Young—who was the subject of national interest, if not admiration—and in the process grew into a celebrity in her own right.

Ann Eliza Webb was born in 1844, the youngest of five children, to Mormon parents who were early converts to the church. She would later say that the church as she knew it in adulthood was different from the simple and sincere religion her parents followed. In the early years Mormons "had not then developed the spirit of intolerance which has since characterized them, and though they were touched with religious fanaticism, they were honest in their very bigotry," she wrote in her book.

Her parents had been Brigham Young's friends since before her birth, although her father was skeptical of church founder Joseph Smith. With Ann Eliza and their other young children, they joined the Latter-day Saints on the trek to Zion.

This lithograph of Ann Eliza Webb Young, made about the time she divorced Brigham Young, was used to publicize her memoir and national public speaking tour.

While Joseph Smith had quietly practiced polygamy in the church's early years, Brigham Young elevated it to an art form after the Saints moved to Utah. Women in Utah saw the chance to marry Brigham Young as an honor—and many of them got the opportunity. Although the number of his wives is still disputed, estimates are that he married at least fifty.

The title of Ann Eliza's book suggests even she didn't know how many wives he had when he married her: She called herself the nineteenth, but it's fairly certain there were at least twenty-seven before her. Some of these temple "sealings" were economic arrangements with women who may not have been able to care for themselves without a husband. In some ways Ann Eliza, a divorcee with two children, fell into this category. In a remote place such as Utah, jobs for single women were scarce. Other women were sealed to Brigham Young for benefits bestowed in the afterlife, with no intention of actually living with him.

Ann Eliza was married at age eighteen to James L. Dee and had two children. She asked for a divorce three years later on the grounds that he was abusive, and she went to live on her parents' farm in Cottonwood, near the mountains at the south end of the Salt Lake Valley. Though her mother—who would be a lifelong ally—didn't like polygamy, Ann Eliza's father did take additional wives.

Brigham Young occasionally visited and told them he had always wanted to marry the pretty and spirited Ann Eliza. On one visit to the Cottonwood farm, he asked her to marry him. She said no, but he told her she would change her mind. Before he left, he told her parents "he hoped they would induce me to listen favorably to his proposal," Ann Eliza wrote in her memoir. "The last remark was made with a peculiar emphasis and a sinister smile, which every saint who had dealings with him knew very well, and whose meaning they also knew. 'Do as I command you, or suffer the weight of my displeasure.'"

She would later say she agreed to marry Young because of his veiled threats against her and her family. But she also thought marriage to Brigham Young would elevate her place in the community (she referred often to her social station) and give her and her family the financial security they had lost. According to her, not only did that not happen, but she was neglected and her children dressed in rags.

She married Brigham Young in 1868; he was sixty-seven and she was twenty-four. After the first year, she didn't live with the rest of the Young family, instead living with her frail mother on a farm outside of town. Ann Eliza said she was banished from the household because of jealousy on the part of Amelia, widely considered Brigham's favorite wife.

Ann Eliza complained that conditions on the farm were barely livable and that he should be ashamed that he gave her so little to live on. Finally, Brigham moved her to a house in the city, but that wasn't enough; she had to take in boarders to keep up her standard of living. Some of them were not Mormon, which gave her a chance to make friends outside the faith who would later help her leave her marriage.

By 1873 Ann Eliza Young had had enough. She packed up her things, moved out of the house, and went to stay at the Walker House hotel. There, she met with lawyers who were gleeful about the prospect of making a bundle—and sticking it to the great Brigham Young.

Ann Eliza created quite a stir when she filed for divorce. Nobody dared say no to Brigham Young, and yet here was a twenty-nine-year-old woman who not only refused to be his wife but was also brave enough— or impudent enough—to ask for alimony. Based on Young's substantial land holdings and at least theoretically sizable income, she asked for a lot: $1,000 a month in support and $20,000 for attorneys' fees.

On July 17 the *New York Times* printed an item describing her departure "carrying off her furniture and personal effects" and calling it "a great sensation." The story continued: "Great revelations are expected concerning the inner domestic life of the Prophet. Mrs. Young is enjoying the sympathy of the Gentile ladies, and polygamous Mormons are a good deal disturbed."

This was unheard of at the time. The few Mormon women who did leave their husbands generally fled to the protection of soldiers the federal government had stationed nearby, or to sympathetic churches of other denominations that were glad to help a woman fleeing from polygamy. They didn't often ask to be compensated for their troubles.

Newspapers nationwide followed the court proceedings. Ann Eliza took the stand against her husband, saying he had never provided well enough for her and her mother and that they were stressed and ill because of it.

Amos Jay Cummings, a reporter for the *New York Sun* who was in Utah at the time, recorded the details of her testimony: "Brigham began a systematic course of neglect, unkindness, cruel and inhuman treatment, finally deserting her, and satisfying her that he no longer entertained the slightest feeling of affection or respect for her," he wrote, going on to report that Ann Eliza claimed her husband appropriated all her earnings from working on the farm and taking in renters.

Brigham Young had no intention of paying up. He testified as well, saying he didn't have as much money as she said he did. Cool and unruffled, he scoffed at the lawsuit, calling it a blackmail attempt and his enemies "murderers and thieves" just like the ones he said had always harassed the Mormons. He never showed any sign of disappointment in being rejected by Ann Eliza; fighting among his wives always irritated him. "I will go into heaven alone, rather than have scratching and fighting around me," he once said.

The divorce case was soon bound up in arguments over jurisdiction and other legal issues. As it made its way through the courts, Ann Eliza knew she had to leave Utah. Even if she was wrong in claiming Mormons might do her harm, the threat of heavy criticism and social ostracism was definitely real. What was a woman to do? Hit the national speaking circuit, of course.

Ann Eliza recounted her dramatic escape that fall: Her father hired a coach to drive her in the middle of the night to a train station north of town so she could avoid running into any of Brigham Young's minions in Salt Lake. She might have been exaggerating; after all, she had been seen around town for the preceding three months and nothing bad had happened. Then again, she had said she feared the Mormons might kidnap her.

She went to Denver, then on to Washington, D.C. She wasn't alone. Having been excommunicated from Mormonism, she joined the Methodist church. One of the Methodist activists she met was Major James B. Pond, who would later become an agent for famous speakers like Mark Twain and Booker T. Washington. He called her story "the most interesting and thrilling story that anybody ever heard."

As soon as her story hit the national press, she started getting invitations to speak in lecture halls and churches around the country. Pond offered to be her booking agent, and she, in turn, helped him attract more high-profile clients. In fact, many of the people helping her had something to gain—the lawyers, the anti-polygamy Methodists, even the federal courts. They knew her story could only help their side in the battle over polygamy. "Our people decided that if Ann Eliza could tell that story in Washington, we would get some attention and legislation," Pond later wrote.

It helped that she was a sympathetic character—young, pretty, and articulate. "I have never found so eloquent, so interesting, so earnest a talker," Pond wrote in his memoirs. When she went to meet James G. Blaine, the Speaker of the U.S. House of Representatives, he was impressed by her composure and her cause. Soon, Pond recalled, "that room was packed with members of Congress. There was a stampede on the floor, and she held an ovation for two hours." Congress passed the Poland Bill, which called for stricter prosecution of polygamy, shortly thereafter.

To an audience already titillated by Mormons and polygamy, Ann Eliza's story symbolized all that was both interesting and shocking about Utah. Just how powerful was Brigham Young, and what was he like in person? What was it like to live in polygamy? Did Mormons really go along with all this wholeheartedly, or were they under some kind of powerful spell? How would the courts decide her challenge?

As it turned out, the law would not work entirely in her favor. One court ordered Brigham Young to pay a lesser amount in alimony than she had requested and held him in contempt when he didn't, even jailing him overnight for failure to pay. He didn't think he should have to pay alimony, but even if he was ordered to, he said, he had more than sixty people to support and didn't have the money. When he still refused to pay, the court ordered that some of his possessions be sold off to raise cash. But few Mormons could bring themselves to participate in such an unseemly auction, and it only raised $1,200.

Finally, the court determined that—as Brigham Young had shrewdly argued—Ann Eliza was never legally married to him. Thus, she couldn't claim alimony. The courts, which had declared over and over that laws against polygamy should be enforced, had no choice but to apply that same standard to her.

Ann Eliza didn't get her divorce decree. On the other hand, the court said, she and Brigham did obviously have some relationship, so it let the previous demand for compensation stand. It wasn't nearly what she had hoped for. But by this time she was busy with a new life, giving lectures all over the United States and Canada with barely time to breathe between engagements. Ann Eliza's mother continued to live with Eliza and her two sons, as she would until her death in 1884.

In 1875, with encouragement from her activist friends (who probably helped her write it), Ann Eliza decided to tell the story of her life in a book. She was not the only one to do this: Fanny Stenhouse, a Mormon convert who left the church in 1869, literally wrote a "tell-all" book about Mormonism. *Tell It All: A Woman's Life in Polygamy* has the distinction of being co-written by *Uncle Tom's Cabin* author Harriet Beecher Stowe, who regarded polygamy on par with slavery.

The subtitle to *Wife No. 19—The Story of a Life in Bondage, Being a Complete Exposé of Mormonism, and Revealing the Sorrows, Sacrifices and Sufferings of Women in Polygamy*—sums up Ann Eliza's premise. Weighing in at more than 600 pages, it is a detailed and entertaining blow-by-blow dissection of her life up to that point, including the divorce proceedings, richly illustrated with dozens of drawings.

The book was much more than an autobiography. It also gave a history of the church's early years, as Ann Eliza understood them, including how polygamy came to be part of church doctrine. She wanted "to impress upon the world what Mormonism really is; to show the pitiable condition of its women, held in a system of bondage that is more cruel than African slavery ever was, since it claims to hold body and soul alike," as she wrote in the book. "I have consecrated myself to the work, not merely for my own sake, but for the sake of all the unhappy women of Utah, who, unlike myself, are either too powerless or too timid to break the fetters which bind them."

The book discussed some of the church's most secretive and controversial matters, including the existence of "Danite" squads of Mormon enforcers who she said raided the countryside, stealing from and attacking Mormons' neighbors. She said it seemed every time a church leader faced disobedience from his followers, he conveniently had a "revelation" that what he was doing was the will of God. Followers didn't dare question policies they felt could have come from God himself.

Ann Eliza's writing is dramatic, opinionated, and sprinkled with some dark humor. She had no qualms about detailing her opinions of well-known Mormons, living or dead. She called Joseph Smith a "libertine" and said he initiated polygamy not as a result of a divine command but as a way to be as promiscuous as he wanted.

She mocked Brigham Young's 1852 declaration making polygamy an official part of church doctrine, saying "its language is as ungrammatical as its tendency is immoral." She said he was "entirely uneducated, and had been noted for nothing except his fidelity to the Prophet [Joseph Smith] and the church and his hard-working disposition. But he was shrewd enough to see his opportunity and to seize it, and yet to do it in such a manner that neither his associates nor the church itself had the least suspicion of his real plan."

At the end of her book, she listed church officials and discussed their backgrounds, calling Daniel H. Wells—second counselor to Brigham Young and husband of Emmeline Wells—"one of the most cruel, bigoted, and tyrannical men in Utah."

Others had written about the perils of polygamy, but no one wrote from such a place of authority. In one of the book's prefaces, John B. Gough wrote, "From her experience and the sufferings she has endured, she is fully competent to expose the whole system, and show to the public the true side of it, as no other person can or will."

She knew her book would not endear her to Mormons—and especially not plural wives. In the book she wrote a note to her sister wives, acknowledging their feelings and motivations. But any tenderness she felt toward them wasn't enough to make her back down, as she wrote in her book's introduction:

> *I think of you often with the sincerest sympathy for your help-less condition, bound to a false religion and fettered by a despotic system; and I wish from the depths of my heart that I could bring you, body and soul, out from the cruel bondage, and help you to find the freedom, rest, and peace which have become so sweet to*

me since my eyes have been opened to the light of a true and com-
forting faith.

Since I have left Utah, I know that some of you have cen-
sured me severely, and have joined in personal denunciations.
But I know that you are actuated by a mistaken zeal for the cause
which you feel yourselves bound to sustain. You, no doubt, regard
my course with horror. I look upon your lives with pity.

The other wives were not impressed with her words, nor were they happy when Ann Eliza included details of their lives in her book. They severely and publicly criticized her, as they had since she left the marriage two years earlier.

In 1883 Ann Eliza married Moses R. Denning, a man she met at one of her lectures, and moved to Michigan. After giving an estimated 1,000 speeches all over the country, Ann Eliza settled down to married life. But like the first two, this marriage would not end happily: The couple divorced in 1893.

In the following years Ann Eliza, once such a sparkling figure on the national stage, slid into sadness and obscurity. Her dear mother was dead. Her sons had grown and moved away (both would die of tuberculosis). Her father died in 1903. Her book, once so popular it required several reprints, was hardly selling; by this time, the Mormons had given up polygamy, diminishing interest in her story.

No one knows how Ann Eliza ended her days. No one heard anything from her after 1908, when a new version of her book was printed. That has proved a frustration to years of biographers since, including Irving Wallace, who did extensive research for his historical novel, the *Twenty-Seventh Wife,* which is closely based on her life. That book, published in 1961, brought the celebrated and tragic figure of Ann Eliza alive for a new generation and helped ensure her lasting fame, as did another novel, David Ebershoff's *The 19th Wife:*

A Novel, published in 2008. Clearly, her story has a lasting power to captivate.

For their part, many Mormons saw Ann Eliza as a lying traitor. After Wallace wrote his book, Mormon writer Hugh Nibley used Ann Eliza's story as a case study in how non-Mormon writers use inflammatory language, poor scholarship, and outright lies to produce influential but inaccurate portraits of the church. "There is not a scrap of external evidence for any of the horror that surrounds our informant; the outrage never lies in what actually happens, but only in Ann Eliza's very private and very secret *reaction* to it," Nibley seethed.

Was Ann Eliza a disagreeable gold digger who went after Brigham Young's money? Was she a pawn of the forces opposed to Mormonism? Or was she an intelligent, desirable woman who refused to be treated like a servant by her own husband? The truth is probably somewhere in the middle, and we will never have all the answers. Either way, she gave the world a compelling story that helped change history, a story that still intrigues as well as entertains us.

Dora B. Topham
("Belle London")

(1866–ca. 1925)

ENTERPRISING MADAM

Dora B. Topham was smart. She was famous. She was prosperous. She had a reputation for her great business sense. Her only problem was, well, her business. Under her pseudonym, "Belle London," she made her fortune through prostitution.

Belle London didn't look like a stereotypical prostitute. Having been in "management" since she was in her twenties, she dressed and acted more like a school principal in public. She wore high-necked blouses, glasses, and long, dark skirts. She put her hair up in a chignon. Like many famous madams who tried to keep their business and private lives separate, Dora devised an alter ego for her work. "Dora Topham" may not have even been her real name, and she is known to have used at least four aliases in her life. Sex workers often went by different names when they got married, had children, or moved to a new place.

Even those who objected to Belle London's line of work—as most people did—couldn't help but acknowledge her strengths. One newspaper suggested she should try her hand at legitimate business: "She is known to have executive ability of a high order, to be gifted with business acumen above that of many men and most women," it said. "Should she turn her talents to legitimate use she could accomplish much constructive work that would be of benefit to society."

As Utah's population of miners and railroad workers grew, so did the number of prostitutes. While there's plenty of evidence they existed, including both stories and police reports, fewer records remain about the madams themselves.

This photo, taken in about 1908, shows Dora B. Topham at her most dignified. It doesn't hint that at the time, she was Utah's most notorious madam. Used by permission, Utah State Historical Society. All rights reserved.

Unlike women artists, activists, or politicians, these women conducted their business in secret. They were lawbreakers, their neighbors believed they directly contributed to society's ills, and they were not welcome in polite company.

All that may be true, but Utah's madams did fill a niche, and maybe a need—for women who had few options for making money.

Some madams also showed themselves to be shrewd businesswomen. Belle London was one of the best. She triumphed in an era when running a brothel was one of the few business opportunities open to women. Her life also illustrates how difficult it was to police prostitution—a problem Utah had in common with every other place.

Dora B. Topham was born in Illinois in 1866. As with most women who made their living through prostitution, little is known about her early life. She may have worked in Denver before moving to Ogden, where she ran a house called the Fashion. She got her first citation for prostitution in Ogden in 1889. She was a young and handsome woman who knew how to bridge the gap between law-abiding and dark worlds.

Both men and women believed that women should occupy a "separate sphere," away from where men conducted business and politics. Women were also supposed to be morally better than men. Prostitution flew in the face of all these beliefs, and sex workers were seen as "fallen women" who took advantage of men's natural inclinations toward depravity.

All kinds of men, including powerful ones, frequented brothels. That gave madams an unusual degree of access, and even influence. They could blackmail certain people if they had to.

Prostitutes typically went into the profession because they didn't see any other choices, and most lived short, unhappy lives at the bottom of the social ladder. They made little money, were often abused, and didn't have a social network to rely on for financial and personal support. Only a few made a good living.

Some madams were notorious. "Gentile Kate" Flint, for example, won a lawsuit against Salt Lake City, claiming, for one thing, that police had harassed her partly because she opposed polygamy. Later, she was said to have bought Brigham Young's carriage after his death and paraded around in it. Emma Whiting was a successful madam who, along with her husband, owned a building on Main Street.

In Park City, where prostitution was thinly concealed well into the twentieth century, "Mother Urban" ran a popular house of ill repute. Ogden madam Fanny Dawson supposedly led a "Murder Company" that would find men with a lot of cash, lure them in, and steal their money—and sometimes poison them. In Eureka, one of many wild mining towns in western Utah, one fallen woman bit another's nose off in a bar fight over a man.

As a railroad town with less Mormon influence than other places in Utah, Ogden had a reputation for harboring more than its fair share of sin. The transcontinental railroad joined the eastern and western halves of the country just north of Ogden in 1869, leading to a dramatic increase in both passenger and freight traffic.

Many of the men coming into town to work on the railroad and to build and run the infrastructure it spurred were "gentiles," the Mormon term for those not of the faith. Gentiles started arriving in Utah as early as the 1840s, when miners and pioneers heading to California and Oregon used it as a waypoint. Settlers, including military men who established forts to keep an eye on the Mormons, began arriving to stay in the 1860s and 1870s.

Many of the new men in town came from far away, even other countries, so they didn't worry too much about anyone's approval. Some were there to work, some hoped to create families, and some were just passing through. They had money, they had drink, and they were lonely.

In Ogden all this activity centered around Twenty-fifth Street, which had a number of nicknames, including "Sin Alley" and "Two-bit Street."

Its brick storefronts were (and still are) conveniently located right next to the train station, which made it an easy destination for travelers and railroad workers. In back rooms and upper floors, Dora Topham and her women plied their trade, building her business into Ogden's biggest and most profitable house of ill repute.

At first the Mormon settlers responded to prostitution the way people usually did—through prosecution and sometimes violence. But then officials decided it was inevitable and should be regulated instead. Ogden largely overlooked prostitution in Belle London's time, fining the practitioners but rarely arresting them. The fines were more like a tax the women knew would be added to the cost of business.

In Salt Lake City, houses of prostitution were generally on the inside of city blocks, where they couldn't be easily seen. Many of them were downtown along Commercial Street, now Regent Street, a half block east of Main Street. But for a short time, Salt Lake City government leaders experimented with something else: an official, government-sanctioned block of prostitution. And the woman they chose to run it was Belle London.

Salt Lake City's elected officials were from the American Party, a new political party that arose in Utah partly in opposition to polygamy. They sought practical ways to deal with many social problems, including prostitution as well as drinking and gambling. They felt that by creating a new district dedicated to prostitution, they could keep brothels out of respectable neighborhoods. Prostitution would still not be legal, but it wouldn't be prosecuted, as long as it was confined to the "red-light" district.

Police and Mayor John Bransford supported this idea, hoping it would cut down on related violence. Others agreed that "reform houses" for prostitutes didn't work, just as they hadn't for polygamist wives. Besides, officials hoped they could end the cycle in which police essentially turned a blind eye to prostitution in exchange for bribes, and where the city's fines amounted to business fees.

Not everyone liked the idea. Some said the "Stockade," as it came to be called, was nothing more than a state-sponsored "municipal bawdy house." The *Salt Lake Tribune* said it was a "grotesque" idea that showed a "lack of decency and moral perception, to say nothing of common sense." Others said the city should be helping get prostitutes out of the life, not enabling them and their patrons. The sheriff, who originally supported the idea, turned against it and refused to help—a decision that got him fired.

Despite opposition, the city and a group of investors, the innocuous-sounding Citizen's Investment Company, bought up land in the block between 100 and 200 South and 400 and 500 West, just west of downtown (now the site of a shopping mall called the Gateway). It was near the railroad tracks and away from "legitimate" storefronts. It was also in a neighborhood mostly composed of working-class immigrants, who were insulted at the notion that their neighborhood would be an ideal location for a block of brothels. They launched a lawsuit against the city.

The sex workers did business in low-slung brick buildings divided into small rooms, or "cribs," on two sides of the block and lived in housing on the other two. The block's use was clear to anyone who looked on.

The city and investors chose Dora Topham to run the operation. Why her? Maybe because she provided a significant portion of the upfront costs—reportedly, the "notorious woman of Ogden" put $20,000 toward the venture. She had already shown herself to be adept at working with local politicians and police. She was also a smart business owner, having run a successful brothel for twenty years. Since money was coming from investors as well as government coffers, it was important to bring in someone with business acumen and an ability to handle finances. To help avoid legal as well as financial liability, she and her partners set up a separate company that technically owned the Stockade.

She was also reputed to be good to her employees, unlike some madams who could be abusive or greedy to their subordinates. Belle London kept a home for her "fallen" women, which served as a hospital when they were sick. She also had women checked by doctors when they first came to work for her.

She later told a newspaper that she never liked or wanted to be in the business of prostitution. "My conscience—yes, I have a conscience—has troubled me about it a good many times," she said, but added, "I can do this much: I can make the business as clean as it is possible for such a business as this to be, and I can persuade a great many girls who are just starting in a life of shame to travel other paths...."

Thus, Dora became the only state-sanctioned madam in Utah history. That designation gave her power over dozens of women and their businesses. It also put her fellow madams in an even more precarious position than usual. When the Stockade opened, police told brothel operators elsewhere in the city to close up shop and stepped up prosecution of other brothels.

Dora invited the city's other madams to join her at the Stockade. One newspaper account said she had offered a generous sum to workers who would relocate and convince their fellow madams to lease property in the district and pay fees to Dora. The paper quoted Dora as saying, "I will protect you with my life, if need be. I know what I am talking about and want women to show the others in Salt Lake that this place will not be molested." Clearly, she was a woman with connections as well as a lot of self-confidence.

She could also be ruthless. One downtown madam, in appealing her prostitution conviction, said she was harassed and eventually arrested by police working in league with Dora after the madam refused to join the others at the Stockade.

By 1909 as many as 170 women were working at the Stockade at any given time. While some of them moved from downtown, many of them were recruited from outside Salt Lake City. For her time, Dora was an equal-opportunity employer: Some of the women, including at least one of the madams, were Black; others were Asian or Latina. Dora was taking in significant cash in payments for rent (which she collected daily), royalties, and markups on items such as liquor. For all intents and purposes, the Stockade was a company town, and Dora was its CEO.

She also supervised security and kept track of the women's whereabouts; anyone wanting to leave the Stockade or make big changes in their business had to get permission from "Miss Belle." Although arrests decreased dramatically during its existence, some women from the Stockade were still fined. Belle London bailed them out of jail, and no matter how many of them got into trouble, she continued operating. She also met with local leaders to promote the idea of controlled prostitution, using her considerable charm and distinguished bearing to try to win them over.

But as the face of the Stockade, she was vulnerable. Everyone knew who ran the operation, and everyone knew she had friends in the government and police forces. If they lost power, she would lose their protection.

The American Party's opponents in Salt Lake City, both Mormon and not, were vocally appalled by the Stockade. Complaints also came from the state and county as well as church, business, and civic groups. Anti-polygamy activists turned more of their attention to prostitution after polygamy lost official Mormon church support and began declining. Like polygamy, prostitution concerned sex—which made it all the more outrageous.

Some madams refused to leave their property and independent businesses downtown, which meant the Stockade didn't succeed in removing prostitutes from the central business district. With the women moving in from out of town, it seemed there were more sex workers in town than ever. And even while it had the approval of the city's mayor, any kind of prostitution was still technically illegal.

In June of 1909 Salt Lake County sheriff's deputies raided the Stockade and arrested forty-two women. Dora turned herself in and declared the Stockade closed, and charges against her were dropped. Her employees were forced to fend for themselves. One of the American Party's detractors asked how an honorable man such as Mayor Bransford could "invite the Belle of Ogden to transplant her Cyprian empire to the town in which he has his home?"—implying that prostitution was an activity apparently better left to less law-abiding towns such as Ogden.

Although his opponents used the Stockade extensively in their campaign against him, Bransford won reelection, and the following March it reopened with Belle London once again heading the venture. Once again neighbors protested. And once again the police didn't do much to stop her.

This time newspapers reported that Belle London had decided to use her opponents' own words in her arguments for her business. She invited some of the city's prominent reformers to visit her offices in Ogden as well as some of her parlor houses. They were more nicely appointed than most; then again, the madam likely made sure they would look their best for the occasion. She told her guests she tried to steer women away from prostitution, but if they insisted on living that life, she took them in and made sure they did it in the safest and most sanitary way possible. She made sure she only hired women over eighteen who were determined to be prostitutes anyway. She also told them she herself didn't do any of the dirty work and that she hoped her daughter would take over after her.

If Belle London thought this would win over her enemies, she was wrong. The city attorney charged her with prostitution, but when police went to arrest the prostitutes, they had been alerted (some of the security officers were off-duty policemen) and the Stockade was empty. And when Dora went to court, sympathetic jurors acquitted her on one charge, and the rest were dismissed. She again promised to close up shop, and again, she didn't.

Though the city attorney tried again to shut her down, again he failed—partly because she had set the business up in such a way that it was impossible to prove she was its owner. He finally admitted defeat, saying no jury would convict anyone in conjunction with the Stockade.

Her ability to stay in business is also evidence of her close working relationship with the (male) politicians of her time, in an era when women were not supposed to operate in the man's "sphere of influence."

Dora Topham's downfall came not from a man but through another woman.

In 1911 state legislators changed laws to make it illegal for anyone to entice a woman into prostitution, even if that woman had already worked as a prostitute. Such laws were on the books but had only applied to "chaste" women. Previously, women who had already "fallen" were apparently lost causes. A woman named Helen Lofstrom said another woman had kidnapped her daughter and taken her to the Stockade, where Helen rescued her with the help of a male friend and a revolver.

The ensuing court case revealed that Dora Topham not only knew the "victim" but may have broken up her mother's marriage years before. The court ruled that the young woman was working at the Stockade voluntarily, but under the new law, that didn't help Dora. While the case was going on, it also emerged that Dora had tried to bribe Mrs. Lofstrom and her daughter to keep them from testifying, so it's hard to say what the truth was.

Although a number of people—including some police—came forward to vouch for Dora Topham's good character, she was found guilty. Facing the possibility of a long prison sentence, she closed the Stockade permanently. She vowed to continue working on behalf of women and asked the female anti-prostitution activists to help. "I am aware that my action will turn upon the streets a large number of women who will not know where to go," she said.

The reformers did offer help to any woman who wanted to go straight, but few took them up on it. They couldn't make as much money working as domestic servants—essentially the only respectable jobs open to single women—and they didn't want to give up the power conferred by their jobs as prostitutes.

Belle London was sentenced to eighteen years of hard labor. The district attorney who prosecuted her case ran for mayor. Though he didn't win, neither did John Bransford. That election spelled doom for the American Party, partly based on its support for the Stockade.

Dora Topham took her case to the Utah State Supreme Court, which overturned her conviction. But without allies in city government, she knew better than to make another try at the Stockade.

But Dora wasn't about to give up on the business that had proved so lucrative, the only profession she had ever known. She moved back to Ogden and operated brothels there and in Salt Lake City until she moved to California a few years later.

Despite efforts by some to curb the "unseemly" behavior, brothels continued to operate and were especially persistent in places like Ogden and Park City; the cribs on Twenty-fifth Street, for example, didn't shut down until World War II.

Although she retired, faded out of the news, and died in California, Dora Topham left a distinctive mark on Utah. According to some accounts, her ghost still haunts Ogden's Twenty-fifth Street, the place that launched one of the most notorious careers in Utah history.

Martha Hughes Cannon

(1857–1932)

DOCTOR AND POLITICAL LEADER

When traveling British sociologist and reformer Beatrice Webb arrived in Salt Lake City in 1898, there was one female resident she most wanted to meet: the woman famous for beating her husband in a race for the Utah state senate. When she went to the woman's house, she found "a sprightly pleasant-looking little person with energetic gait and decided manner," who recounted the story, recalling how her husband had asked her the day before the race: "Now how do you expect to come out, my girl?"

Obviously, she came out well: Martha Hughes Cannon not only beat her husband but was elected the nation's first female state senator in the process.

The visitor couldn't help but ask about one of the other things that had defined Martha Cannon's life: the practice of polygamy. The answer, Webb wrote: "It was an enormous advantage, she asserted, for a woman to be able to select a really good man to father her children instead of putting up with any miserable fellow who might be left over by other women." The energetic little woman went on, saying, "It gave the women more real physical freedom: if they chose, they could have had an independent life; they were not completely absorbed as one wife is by her husband."

Webb was impressed, recalling in her memoirs that "We left our vivacious frank little senator with regret; she was such a self-respectful and vigorous pure-minded little soul: sensitive yet unself-conscious, indiscreet yet loyal."

Martha Hughes Cannon is one of the most respected women in Utah history. She became a doctor when few women did. Like many Mormon

Martha Hughes Cannon was elected to the Utah Senate in 1896, defeating her own husband in the process. Used by permission, Utah State Historical Society. All rights reserved.

women of her time, she practiced polygamy and publicly defended the practice, even as she had private reservations. As the fourth wife of a Mormon church official, she had to flee the state and then the country to avoid prosecution. But she is most famous as the first woman elected to a state senate, winning an election against several contestants including her own husband. Later, she served on the Utah State Board of Health and drafted some of the state's first health regulations.

All this could only have been accomplished by an intelligent, active woman—especially since this woman didn't come from privilege and never did anything the easy way, even when she could have.

Martha Maria Hughes was born in Wales in 1857, a year before her family emigrated to the United States to join their fellow members of the Church of Jesus Christ of Latter-day Saints. On their trek across the plains to Utah, Martha's mother, Elizabeth, walked most of the way so her ailing husband could ride in the wagon. When her shoes wore out, she tied her feet with rags and kept walking. Martha's father, who had been ill for years, died three days after reaching Utah in 1861. One sister also died along the way to "Zion."

Elizabeth remarried and had five more children, making for a combined family of eleven children. Her precocious daughter Martha held her own. "Mattie" went to work as a schoolteacher by age fourteen and then as a typesetter for local publications including the *Woman's Exponent,* the magazine for Mormon women. Even as a young woman, she always wanted to help others, so she set her sights on becoming a doctor. At a time when few women studied medicine and even fewer schools offered to teach it to them, it was a high goal. She started saving money for medical school and pursued undergraduate studies at the University of Deseret in Salt Lake City.

She was about to get help. Mistrust of "gentile" doctors and a high disease rate prompted church leader Brigham Young to encourage interested faithful to head back east for medical training. He and Relief Society president Eliza R. Snow called for more women doctors, feeling it was preferable for Mormon women to treat each other, certainly when it came to "female" matters like childbirth. "The time has come for women to come forth as doctors in these valleys of the mountains," Young proclaimed.

At the same time, the medical profession—long based on little more than suspicion, faith, and luck—was using new discoveries and practices and gaining credibility. Midwives had always been a part of the Mormon social fabric, but medicine was advancing, and people in Utah, like people everywhere, wanted access to the most up-to-date treatments.

When Martha was accepted into medical school at the University of Michigan (one of the few that admitted women), church leaders officially lent their approval for her education, and the church gave her financial assistance. To make ends meet during medical school, she washed dishes and did housekeeping. After medical school she did postgraduate work in science and pharmacy at the University of Pennsylvania, where she was the only woman in a class of seventy-five. She also studied oratory, or public speaking, at the National School of Oratory. That skill would come in handy later in her life.

Martha was one of several women who would become prominent doctors in Utah. Intrepid ladies such as Romania Pratt and Ellis Reynolds Shipp were among the vanguard of women leaving Utah to study medicine. Ellis Shipp was a polygamous wife with young children when she went to medical school in Pennsylvania in 1875. Like Martha, she worked odd jobs through school, taking in sewing and even working as the nighttime security guard who kept an eye on the medical school's cadavers! When she returned, Ellis Shipp founded the School of Nursing and Obstetrics. Today a University of Utah medical building is named for her.

Martha returned to Utah in 1882 and practiced medicine, specializing in women's health and pediatrics. She was an independent businesswoman with a private practice, traveling to care for patients, and she was known as both professional and practical. She carried nice shoes to work but wore men's boots when walking distances.

Martha was a good-looking, well-dressed woman, with a soft, pleasant face. She attracted plenty of male attention. She had suitors in her university days, but her hectic schedule and determination didn't leave her much time for frivolity. She wanted someone as mature as she was, and she found him in Angus Munn Cannon, who oversaw all the Mormon congregations in Salt Lake City. He also already had three wives and was twenty-three years her senior. She got to know him when she was the resident physician at the Deseret Hospital in Salt Lake City and he was on the hospital board. They were married in 1884.

It might seem irrational for a woman so capable, intelligent, and emotionally and financially independent to marry a man she would have to share with other women—women whose households her income would likely end up supporting. But she genuinely loved Angus. He was known for his magnetic personality, but she also loved his dedication to the church, which matched her own fierce belief in its truth.

His status as a church leader appealed to her as well, and she knew he shared her convictions in its teachings. That included the doctrine of polygamy. An estimated 10 to 20 percent of Mormons—usually men in leadership positions or from prominent families—practiced polygamy. Martha believed it was an order from God, and that adherence to the law of polygamy was a sign of faith, obedience, and selflessness.

But like many women who privately believed in polygamy and publicly defended it, she sometimes wondered if it wasn't just a trial God gave women to test their faith. In one letter to her husband, Martha wrote, "If we ever live through this present strait, I trust we will be 'wiser and better men' and women. . . . I grow heartily sick and disgusted with it—polygamy."

In public she pointed out polygamy's benefits, saying polygamous wives had more free time. A woman with three sister wives, she reasoned, only had to take care of her husband one week a month. She could choose to marry the best man around, not just whoever was single and available.

The decision to support polygamy was not only personally wrenching but even potentially dangerous. The American government was cracking down on the practice, and in 1874 the Poland Act gave the federal government power to enforce anti-polygamy laws. Authorities investigated and arrested some Mormon men and promised to find and prosecute polygamists even if they didn't live together. Although men were typically the ones jailed for being polygamists, women could be interrogated about their intimate lives and jailed if they refused to testify. The fear of prosecution drove some families into hiding.

Government officials decided to make an example of several church leaders, including Angus Cannon. He was arrested for practicing polygamy three months after his marriage to Martha and was still in jail when their first child, Elizabeth, was born.

Women in Utah publicly protested enforcement of the anti-polygamy law and sent an open letter to President Grover Cleveland in 1886. That year Martha Cannon decided she had to flee from authorities, for her own sake and the sake of her family. She had hidden from authorities a couple of times before when her husband was charged with polygamy, and she didn't want to be called to testify against him.

With her seven-month-old daughter in tow, she fled to England, where she had relatives who would take her in. She left in dramatic fashion. In a story she would often tell later, she was recognized at one train station and had to run to another, leaving her baggage behind (letters from the United Kingdom record her replacing items from the bags, which she never saw again).

She traveled and worked, spending much of the next two years in England or on the East Coast. She carried on even after some in England realized she was a supporter of polygamy and turned against her.

"I would rather be a stranger in a strange land and be able to hold my head up among my fellow beings than be a sneaking captive at home," she said.

While she was away, she wrote letters to Angus, calling him pet names like "My Own Dear Lover." They both used pseudonyms for themselves and others in case the letters were intercepted by authorities. She missed him and after a while felt she could truthfully tell a grand jury she didn't meet any conditions of being considered someone's wife—a veiled complaint about spending so little time with her husband.

She sometimes got angry, until her husband chastised her and reiterated his love. She promised to keep trying to live "the principle" of polygamy. "I am thankful that God so ordained my destiny to embrace the celestial principle of marriage when I did. And now in it, my energies shall be bent toward its continuance, but I greatly feel my weakness at times, and I know not how long I will hold out in the great Cause," Martha wrote.

She also sympathized with other women in polygamy. "Of course I am only one of hundreds who are like situated, only many of them worse, I fear. But the knowledge that it is *God's plan* to prove them is the only thing that saves them from despair—almost madness I fear."

She felt she had to make sure her husband didn't go to jail, since she thought it was important for him to be able to do his church duties and support the family. Her priorities were always church first, then family, then personal desires. She felt a sense of pride, maybe almost self-righteousness, about leaving her husband for the good of the family even as his other wives remained with him in Utah, and even as he took two more.

Things weren't getting any better for polygamists at home. In 1887 Congress passed the Edmunds-Tucker Act. It required polygamist wives to testify against their husbands and rescinded a woman's right to vote in local elections, a power the state government had granted them in 1870.

Martha returned from abroad in 1888. When she came back to Utah, she revived her private practice and set up a nursing school, making use of her degree and new information she had gathered on visits to nursing schools in Boston, New York, and Europe.

Mormons were eager for statehood and tired of fighting the federal government, which by this time was threatening to ensure that no Mormon, polygamist or not, would ever get the vote. The year that Martha left for San Francisco, 1890, church president Wilford Woodruff issued a "Manifesto" officially ending church support for polygamy and opening the door to statehood.

Now that the Utah territory had mollified the federal government by agreeing to no more polygamous marriages, prosecutions of existing marriages declined. Once again free to pursue her medical career in Utah, Martha returned again in 1892.

Whether at home or traveling, she kept up professional and personal roles. One of them was as a leader of the fight for women's voting rights. She joined the Territorial Suffrage Association, an arm of the National Woman Suffrage Association. She attended the national Women's Conference held in 1893, in conjunction with the Columbian Exposition, and gave a speech about women in Utah. She felt women were good for politics because, as she put it simply, "women are better than men."

In 1896 Utah ratified a state constitution (in which polygamy was forever banned) and held its first elections as a state, with women once again able to vote. The Democratic party asked Martha Cannon to run for the newly created state senate. At the same time, the Republicans asked her husband, Angus, to run on their side. Some people thought Martha would drop out rather than run against her husband—but those people didn't know Martha very well. While she wasn't happy about running against him, she was more upset by the fact that Emmeline Wells was also running. Although they were both leaders in the suffrage movement, Martha wasn't particularly friendly with Emmeline.

Any of the three could have won; there were five contested seats and ten candidates. But the Democrats—including Martha—swept all five, which meant she not only became a state senator but also beat her husband to get the seat.

As the nation's first female state senator, she gained national prominence and used that to speak on behalf of the national suffrage movement, including addressing Congress in 1898. Her passionate speeches were received with acclaim and applause. A Chicago newspaper called her "the brightest exponent of the women's cause in the United States."

During her tenure she was most interested in bills relating to public health and wrote Utah's first sanitation laws. She was appointed a member of the State Board of Health and the State School for the Deaf, Dumb and Blind. She also worked in the treatment of drug addiction.

She retired from the senate in 1899, when her third child, Gwendolyn, was born. Martha was forty-two. She moved to Los Angeles to live with her son in 1927, but she was far from finished with her career. At age seventy she was a staff member of the Graves Clinic there.

Even after her death in 1932, Martha Hughes Cannon remained a model of compassion, determination, and faith. A scholarship at the University of Utah and a government health building in Salt Lake City were named for her. A statue of her stands in the Utah State Capitol rotunda, a steadfast reminder that with enough determination, a woman can achieve even the highest of goals.

SUSANNA BRANSFORD EMERY
HOLMES DELITCH ENGALITCHEFF

(1859–1942)
UTAH'S SILVER QUEEN

Utah's "Silver Queen" was a vivacious and sophisticated figure in the Gilded Age's elite social scene. Having scrambled up from humble roots into an aristocracy that favored "old money," she was always prepared to defend herself against a threat to her station.

When some of her enemies tried to hurt her image by publicly mentioning that she had once been a seamstress in a mining town, she went into action and hired a genealogist to draw up a family tree showing ties to English royalty. The blue-blood link was guaranteed to outweigh the disapproval of biddies who looked down their noses at this outspoken usurper. For the Silver Queen, it seemed, the right amount of money could solve just about any problem.

Susanna Bransford—more precisely, Susanna Bransford Emery Holmes Delitch Engalitcheff—survived deaths of four husbands, partied with the rich and famous, and created a tumultuous life centered around the astonishing wealth she acquired at the height of Utah's mining boom. She was a smiling socialite, a woman the *Salt Lake Tribune* described as "a blend of grand dame, business woman, cosmopolite and breezy westerner, forming a striking and attractive combination." But she also privately suffered great losses and struggled to portray herself in the right social light, battling a gnawing fear that someday she would have to give up the life she felt was her right.

Only in the West, at least in theory, could a young woman leap out of obscurity and become one of the richest people in the country. Hers

Park City silver mines made Utah's "Silver Queen" one of the country's wealthiest women, a status she relished. Used by permission, Utah State Historical Society. All rights reserved.

is the kind of quintessential Old West rags-to-riches tale that becomes legend even as the details of her life are warped and forgotten.

We might know more about Utah's Silver Queen now if, like her contemporary the "unsinkable" Molly Brown, she had been a passenger on the *Titanic* or run for office. She was often in the news, but she carefully controlled her persona and even made up fanciful stories about her life while ignoring aspects of it that displeased her. Because of that, and because she ordered all her personal papers destroyed after her death, her life is literally legendary. Even her wealth itself is a matter of speculation: When she died, people said she had spent a hundred million dollars, but that, too, was probably an exaggeration.

Susanna Bransford was born in Missouri and crossed the plains to northern California with her family, former Confederate sympathizers fleeing the Civil War, in 1864. "Susie" grew up in northern California, one of six children in a family hoping to improve its social standing. Tall and attractive, with thick chestnut hair, she roughhoused with the local boys but also briefly went to finishing school in San Francisco when her family could afford to send her. In one of the stories she liked to tell, robbers stopped a stagecoach she was riding in and were about to rob it until one of the would-be thieves recognized her as an old hometown friend and refused to take her money.

Susanna's family struggled to earn a living, and like Scarlett O'Hara in *Gone with the Wind,* she vowed that she would never be poor as an adult. But unlike a stereotypical socialite, she never married for money. As far as anyone knew, she didn't need to: Her legendary charm seemed to attract money the same way it attracted male admirers.

At twenty-five, having turned down any marriage offers she might have gotten from several romantic entanglements, Susanna moved to Park City, thirty-five miles east of Salt Lake City, and worked as a seamstress while she lived with family friends who owned a general store. She fell in love with the local postmaster, Albion Emery; they were among many working-class citizens trying to make a living in any way they could. A charming fellow in his late thirties, he had (generally unsuccessfully) tried his hand at mining-related jobs in various places throughout northern Utah. They were married in 1884, and he went to work as a bookkeeper. In 1889 they adopted a young orphan named Grace.

Few places were as ripe for a success story as Utah's Wasatch Mountains, where miners were feverishly digging into slopes while speculators tried to plot out the next vein. Utah's first successful prospectors were soldiers the federal government sent to Utah to keep an eye on the Mormons. Brigham Young told his followers not to put their efforts into mining, since he feared it would detract from building "Zion" and encourage outsiders to come to Utah.

When the transcontinental railroad joined the eastern and western sides of America together in 1869, mine owners could transport ore all over the country, and silver's value meant areas rich in it were seething with activity. By the late 1880s Park City's population was booming—and by the turn of the twentieth century, it had 10,000 residents, more than it had as it went into the twenty-first.

Utah's early miners, individuals who prospected their own claims, were overtaken by corporations. Like most of the town's eventual millionaires, Albion Emery made his fortune investing in one of those companies. He bought a share in Park City's Mayflower Mine, which later merged with another mine and became the famed Silver King.

Very quickly, the mine produced piles of ore, and the owners' share values skyrocketed. Over the years, the Silver King would fund Susanna's dreams of wealth and better social standing. Some might have called this a lucky break, but she considered it something of a birthright she inherited from her upper-crust Southern ancestry.

Making his own bid for social prominence, Albion Emery won election to the Territorial House of Representatives and was eventually voted speaker, the first who wasn't Mormon. By this time the mine was earning the Emerys an estimated thousand dollars a day—a good thing, since the couple went on a spending spree that included travel to California and Hawaii.

They moved to Salt Lake City in 1893, and Susanna went to work decorating, entertaining, and working her way into the growing nouveau-riche elite. It was a role she relished—and one she was well suited for with her sparkling personality, expensive tastes, and statuesque good looks.

But things weren't going to be that easy. In 1894 Albion died (some at the time said his early death was a result of a dissolute lifestyle that included too much drinking). His widow held a grand funeral, ordering Salt Lake City's Masonic temple decorated with thousands of flowers. She invited high-ranking political and business figures to pay their respects and even hired a special train to bring mourners from Park City, the town whose mines made the family's fortunes just a few years earlier.

But Emery left no will, and his widow had to fight for his fortune. That fight escalated when mining tycoon R. C. Chambers sued to get much of the Emerys' money, saying that Emery had acted as Chambers's front to buy into the mine and never repaid him. It's true that a bookkeeper would have had a hard time raising the $8,000 Albion Emery put into the mine, but it also appears that Chambers had previously said Emery paid him back. During a dramatic and well-publicized courtroom battle that eventually went to the state supreme court, Chambers finally admitted perjury, and Susanna won.

Her victory ensured a fortune big enough to keep her living in style, and she did, hosting more parties and climbing the social ranks at home and on the coasts.

In 1899 Susanna married Colonel Edwin Holmes, a businessman and multimillionaire from Chicago who had asked for her hand many times. He gave up asking and simply announced their engagement, to everyone's surprise, during a dinner party with friends. This time she couldn't turn him down.

Like her first, her second marriage was a happy one, with a husband who gave her everything she wanted. The couple traveled to Europe, where they befriended minor royalty. Susanna put her daughter, Grace, in a Washington, D.C., boarding school, then hit the party circuit, hobnobbing with New York and Washington, D.C., elites including the Astors and Vanderbilts and making a name for herself as one of the most talked-about socialites in the country.

National newspapers and magazines followed the exploits of "Utah's Silver Queen" with juicy (and sometimes overblown) stories about her. The public read about her travels, the people she met—apparently including Pope Leo XIII—and the dresses and jewels she wore. Reports of the time describe her as outgoing and friendly, but she rarely divulged her true feelings, and she never shared most of her personal papers. She did respond defiantly to anything negative said, printed, or implied about her. After her first husband's death and the court battle that followed, she had decided she would need a thick skin.

In 1901 Colonel Holmes bought his wife the famed Gardo House, one of Salt Lake City's most opulent homes. Mormon leader Brigham Young had it built for his favorite wife, Amelia, years earlier. Susanna hired a Chicago decorator to fill the four-story granite and stucco house, sometimes called "Amelia Palace," with lavish furnishings.

At a time when appearances were paramount, the house reflected the highest of ambitions: It was decorated with ornate furniture, rose and gold brocade, ceiling frescoes, and animal-skin rugs. Visitors walked through wrought-iron metal gates, along a path lit by electric tea lights, up stone steps, and into an entryway dominated by a grand, curving staircase hand-carved out of black walnut.

The house also featured a bubbling indoor water fountain from Tiffany, vases of fresh flowers, five pianos (though Susanna didn't play), and, of course, lots of silver. In 1904 Mr. and Mrs. Holmes had an entire wing, comprising a ballroom and art gallery, added to the house. They invited 400 guests to its grand opening party. They also owned a summer home in the Wasatch Mountains' forested foothills, on the Salt Lake Valley's east side, and a California winter estate called El Roble.

The Silver Queen hosted parties with just the right balance of flair and manners to ensure her spot at the top of the social heap. Their friends were local mining magnates (including old friends David Keith and Thomas Kearns, Albion Emery's Silver King partners), government officials (Susanna's brother, John Bransford, was mayor of Salt Lake City), and out-of-town guests.

She joined ladies' clubs, country clubs, and charitable leagues. But she usually kept her generosity quiet, lavishing most of it on her family: She bought houses for her mother and a nephew, spent an unheard-of $100,000 on her younger sister's wedding, and helped a young friend, actress Adele Blood, pursue a Broadway and film career. But the public mostly saw her as a hostess who always knew how to throw a great party.

She handled at least some of her own finances, eventually buying two hotels, partly to serve as homes for her relatives, and gained a reputation for being good at business as well as socially astute. Even as she plowed through her money, she wanted to ensure that there was plenty left.

Susanna was never close to her daughter, who valued solitude and family, not high society. Against her mother's wishes, Grace married Susanna's nephew Wallace, John Bransford's son. The rift between mother and daughter grew into a permanent split after Grace took her half of Albion Emery's fortune with her when she married. When Grace died a few years later, she left Susanna nothing in her will.

Susanna took this personally—and perhaps it was at least partly meant that way. Grace had always felt her mother focused too much on the wrong things. But to Susanna, wealth and social life were more important than just about anything. No matter how much money she had, she could always imagine the cold fingers of poverty grabbing at her.

The thought of losing a fortune, even one that wasn't really hers to begin with, was too much for her. She sued Grace's heirs to get the money back, and lost—a move that didn't endear Susanna to onlookers in Utah or her own family. Susanna never reconciled with many of her relatives, including her brother. Her need for money severed ties to the people who were once closest to her.

After the widely reported scandal over Grace's estate, Susanna and Colonel Holmes sold Gardo House and moved to California. Though it must have been painful, Susanna didn't want to talk about the lawsuit or the split with her family.

More than twenty years of emotional support and stability ended when Edwin Holmes died in 1927. Susanna mourned, but she responded to his death in typical fashion: by moving on. She traveled abroad with wealthy female friends, and when she returned she moved to New York and took up residence at the swanky Plaza Hotel.

Middle-aged now, without her California friends or Utah relatives nearby, she turned to younger male escorts (a common practice for upper-crust women of the day) to shepherd her to social functions. Even as she neared seventy, she liked the attention she felt added to her reputation as a sought-after woman.

In 1930, when she was seventy-one, Susanna married forty-one-year-old Radovan Delitch, a doctor from Serbia. Though the pair said the marriage was for love, Susanna's highbrow friends were probably more scandalized than impressed. Delitch gave up his medical career, and they used her fortune to travel around America (including visits to Utah) and Europe.

But once again, trouble was following the Silver Queen: The Depression and declining silver prices decimated the value of Silver King stock. Though she knew her money couldn't sustain her spending, she couldn't bring herself to cut back.

She and her husband started fighting. When she asked for a divorce, he fell into a deep depression and went to Europe, with her promising to make the divorce final as soon as he returned. Though he had given up his career and was financially dependent on her, it appears he sincerely missed her, not just her money. He boarded a ship to return to America, hoping to make one last appeal—but on the way, he gave up hope. On Christmas Eve in 1932, he wrote a letter despairing over the wife who wouldn't take him back. Then, he hanged himself.

Again, as Judy Dykman recounts in her biography *The Silver Queen,* Susanna showed no public emotion. When the telegram notice of his suicide arrived, while she was lunching at a hotel with her niece, she quietly folded it up and put it away. "In behavior as well as money, one had to keep up appearances," Dykman writes.

Single again, Susanna turned to a former suitor, Nicholas Engalitcheff, a penniless prince whose family was ejected during the Russian Revolution. He did have one thing Susanna didn't: a title. In 1933 they were married in two separate ceremonies (one of which involved placing crowns on both their heads); she was seventy-four and he was fifty-nine. They separated when she learned he was unfaithful, but they remained married—with both of them still living off her dwindling cash reserves.

When the prince died in New York in 1935, she made a public joke out of the unfaithful Russian playboy. She told people he'd died while they were traveling abroad and she'd put his body in storage. Then she made up an elaborate story about hiring a battleship to give him a proper prince's burial at sea. None of it was true.

It was getting harder and harder for the Silver Queen to keep up appearances. She had to sell her home, her art, and her furniture; she replaced the jewelry with fakes. In 1942, with her fortune gone, most of her family distant, and her closest friends dead, Susanna took a handful of pills and went to sleep forever. After her death, legends lived on, including one that said she still had hidden millions when she died.

She left no money to her family; what little there was went to friends. She told her family that the reason she wasn't leaving them anything was because wealth led to misery. This might have been another ruse to make people think she had more than she did. But she might also have meant it. When she had money, she flaunted it. But her hunger for acceptance and security ultimately cost her both those things. In a lifetime of outrageous good fortune combined with very bad luck, she seized her fate, lived on her own terms, and felt entitled to the heights of success—and sometimes paid a steep price for it.

Maude Adams

(1872–1953)

THE ORIGINAL PETER PAN

Just about everyone knows the story of Peter Pan. But aside from the character's creator, James M. Barrie, nobody knew Peter the way Maude Adams did.

That's because for hundreds of nights onstage, Maude was Peter Pan. One of the best-known actresses of her time, she created the role of the boy who would never grow up, one of the most beloved characters in the world of theater.

Every night she would dress as a boy and act in a play that allowed her to fight pirates, lead an army of "lost boys"—and to fly. She once described what it was like to play the role:

Someone had said that the audience plays half of every play; certainly three-fourths of Peter was the audience's doing. And when three-fourths of that audience were below the age of ten, it was an exciting business.

In a tense moment a whispered "Peter!" would float over the footlights, warning of the approach of the wicked Pirate, long before it was time, according to Barrie, for Peter to know; it was hard not to heed that little voice, and let the plot go hang. Again, when it was Peter's turn to pursue the wicked Pirate, there would come wild cries of "Hurry, Peter! Hurry, Peter!" If Peter's heels had been made of lead, the sound of those little voices would have turned them into feathers.

In 1900 Maude Adams dressed for a role as young Napoleon in L'Aiglon, *her first role as a boy. She would make her biggest mark a few years later, playing Peter Pan.* Used by permission, Utah State Historical Society. All rights reserved.

Maude was striking by any era's standards, with large, expressive eyes and a lithe figure. But it was her ability to captivate an audience that got her the part for which she would be most famous.

She was beautiful, she was talented, and she was daring. And acting was in her genes: Her mother, Asenath ("Annie"), was also a successful actor. The daughter of Mormon parents, Annie was a member of the local theater troupe and traveled around the West to appear in shows, literally setting the stage for her daughter's career. The arts were always important in Utah, and Mormons fostered them early on—theaters were among the first public buildings in Salt Lake City.

Maude Ewing Adams Kiskadden (she would always use Adams as her last name) was born in Salt Lake City in 1872 and made her debut in a play with her mother at nine months. She was a professional actress by the time she was five. Before she could even read, she could memorize pages of dialogue by having them read to her. She was, even then, known as dependable and professional. She even discussed details of her contract, once recalling that as a six-year-old she refused a job because the pay was too low.

Maude's mother doted on her, helping the serious little child learn roles and filling her in on the plays' details and backgrounds.

"Little Maudie" gained fame as she went. She traveled all over the West, to mining towns as well as big cities, in front of all kinds of audiences. She spent much of her time in San Francisco, already a big city with rich culture.

But she considered Utah home, and she returned there regularly, sometimes riding a train alone across the plains and deserts from wherever her mother was performing. She always had good things to say about her hometown: "The people of the valley have gentle manners, as if their spirits moved with dignity," she once wrote. "The memory of them, the thought of them and their lovely valley is an anchor in a changing, roving life."

She loved seeing her father and visiting her grandmother, who lived on a farm, and playing with her older brother. Riding horses and sheep was a very different thrill from the one she got being onstage.

Her beloved grandmother was a steadying influence on her childhood and a model of hard work and kindness. She "had the courage of her character; her traditions were all she needed, and she lived by them candidly and stoutly," Maude recalled.

Her father, who worked in banking and mining, wasn't sure he wanted his daughter to follow her mother's profession, but he gave in to his daughter's pleading. He was even less happy about a trip she and her mother took to New York City. Once they arrived in the East, Maude decided he was right, since the towns on the East Coast were gritty and inhospitable. To make things worse, the star of the show made off with the company's box-office proceeds. When they returned to California, Maude vowed to go back and make it on Broadway.

Though she occasionally went to school when she stayed with her grandmother in Utah (her father also split his time between Utah and San Francisco), it bored her. Working as an actress had taught her enough lessons to put her ahead of other children her age, so her family decided to keep her out of school until she was older—which she considered "a very satisfactory decision, opening up vistas of freedom." Rather than learning about things at school, she learned English by appearing in plays by Shakespeare and history by studying for roles.

She was always playing a part—which meant she never really developed her own sense of personal identity. "To make one's own acquaintance is difficult enough under ordinary circumstances; but if life is begun pretending to be Eva, the youthful heroine of 'Uncle Tom's Cabin,' or Little Paul in 'The Octoroon,' or this or that other little boy or girl, it becomes increasingly difficult to separate whom from which," she wrote years later in a magazine essay that looked back on her life. She called this autobiography "The One I Knew Least of All"—referring to herself.

Her father, whom she loved and called "always a faithful ally," died in 1878. It was a loss that grew as the years went on.

By the time she was ten, Maude was a seasoned professional. But it was time to take a break. Maude and her mother returned to Salt Lake City, where the girl studied at the Salt Lake Collegiate Institute (it later became Westminster College), one of Utah's first private schools. It was a popular place for those who wanted to avoid Mormon-dominated public schools.

Annie tried to find some other kind of work in Salt Lake City to be near her daughter but didn't find anything as financially rewarding as acting. It wasn't long before she returned to the theater circuit. Maude always intended to rejoin her. She studied drama, French, dance, and music—all of which would make her a more marketable actor.

Being in school full-time was difficult for precocious Maude. The other children seemed like "a blank wall" to her, and she was annoyed by their immature behavior. Still, she was put in charge of coaching other students in public speaking, and she moved audiences with her elocution skills.

Maude loved Salt Lake City's mountainous landscape and life with her grandmother. But Utah wasn't as fun without her father, and she missed her mother and the stage. The theater was the only home she had ever known, and it was the world her mother inhabited; she couldn't think of one without the other.

She begged to return to the acting world, and her mother finally agreed. She had missed Maude, too, after their years of working as a team on the road. So Maude caught another train to rejoin the acting company on the West Coast.

She returned to the stage facing a big question: Could she make the transition from child star to adult actor?

Then as now, childhood stardom didn't necessarily translate into a lifelong career. Maude later called her first role as a leading lady "a complete failure." She was too small and thin to come across as very womanly. Her performances weren't convincing. Audiences didn't applaud, leaving her to exit the stage in silence after a big solo scene. Another actor advised her to switch to comedy.

Suffering through the harshly critical acting world as well as the usual trials of being a teenager, Maude's self-esteem faltered and she grew horribly self-conscious. But her mother encouraged her to keep going—and pointed out what others had before: Maybe Maude wasn't meant to play serious drama. Standing her daughter in front of a mirror and pointing out Maude's upturned nose, she said, "Look at yourself. Do you think anyone could play tragedy with a nose like that?"

Maude persisted in thinking the only "respectable" theater was tragedy and tried out for serious parts. Her breakout role was in a play called *The Paymaster,* which took their company eastward again. Although the West Coast felt like home, all the truly big names in theater played in New York. Mother and daughter headed there together to seek their fortune.

Life was not easy. They didn't have a lot of money, and they saved by living in cheap boardinghouses near the theaters so they didn't have to pay for transportation. Sometimes, they would go weeks or even months without roles. Always protective, Annie kept a watchful eye on her daughter. In one early play, Maude's character had to jump into a tank of water onstage. Rather than allow Maude to take on the dangerous jump, her mother switched places with her at the last minute during performances.

Maude got a major break when she joined a new company run by Charles Frohman, who was one of the world's most prominent theater producers and who would become her mentor. She worked her way up from secondary to leading parts, moving away from heavy, tragic roles that didn't suit her style.

Maude's work ethic would propel her to stardom and keep her there. She knew anything but the best work wasn't going to get her to the top of her profession, and she was self-critical and honest about the performances she didn't consider up to par. She once wrote:

> *Go for first-rate things. Don't accept from yourself a second-rate sincerity, a second-rate sense of justice. Sometimes it seems that we are successful only because we have not tried hard enough for our best. If we don't compromise, we do the hard thing and we fail. We do the hard thing and we fail. We do the hard thing, and one day we succeed.*

As well as working hard to hone the dramatic part of her craft, she attended every dress rehearsal of every other play she could get to. She was always interested in technology and noted the mechanical workings of every theater she visited, eventually becoming an expert in stage lighting.

Her costar and head of the new company was John Drew, a big-name actor. With her well-honed grace and charm on the stage, as well as a better feel for roles, her popularity started overtaking his. After one show the *New York Times* opined that "Maude Adams, not John Drew, has made the success of 'The Masked Ball' at Palmer's, and is the star of the comedy. Manager Charles Frohman, in attempting to exploit one star, has happened upon another of greater magnitude."

The company's biggest early success was a play based on J. M. Barrie's book *The Little Minister*. The story goes that Barrie was reluctant to allow his book to be made into a play, since he feared no actress could play his lead female character, Miss Babbie. But when he saw Maude onstage in New York, he finally gave his permission.

The play opened in 1897 to huge acclaim, securing Maude's role as a leading lady. She was pretty—maybe more by today's standards than her day's, since her peers regarded her as too thin. Her nuanced, graceful performances, along with her sincerity and warm personality, made her wildly popular with audiences—even when she wasn't with critics.

The admiration was also financially rewarding. At the peak of her career, she was making a reported one million dollars a year, making her the highest-paid actor of her day. A biographer at the time wrote, "Regarded merely as a business proposition, a drawing card, no American star, however much greater her histrionic powers might be, has ever had so tremendous and widespread a popularity as Maude Adams enjoys in the United States today."

Love-struck Americans named everything from dolls to hats to corsets for her. One company created a life-size gold statue of her to represent "The American Girl" at the 1901 Paris Exhibition. It weighed 1,200 pounds and cost an estimated $187,000 to make (plus $12,000 to ship).

On the verge of serious illness from overwork, Maude got away to Europe in 1901 and took a "rest cure," staying at a convent where she gained an affection for the Catholic church that would last the rest of her life. She also saw plays and requested backstage tours of great theaters in Vienna and Paris. When she heard that James Barrie wanted to meet her in person, she eagerly traveled to the biggest theater city of all: London.

She had communicated with Barrie by letter while she acted in *The Little Minister*. And he had long wanted to meet in person the actress who so brilliantly portrayed his heroine.

When she arrived at his house, he came bounding down the stairs with a St. Bernard and asked if Maude would like to see them wrestle. She later wrote that, whatever her idea might have been at the start of it, "the journey from New York to Cherbourg—Paris, Vienna, London—had been taken solely to see that wrestling." By the end of their three-day visit, Maude felt as if she had always known him.

For the next few years, she toured the United States, appearing in many plays, including several by Barrie. She often worked until she physically broke down and had to take time off, sometimes months, to recover.

During one break, she took an exciting trip to Egypt. She loved the continuity of its history; while other countries shuffled governments and borders, "Egypt stayed put," she wrote. "Those thousands of years seemed to give assurance, certainly of centuries to come; there seemed nothing in the world but time." Traveling with a group of female friends, she saw the Pyramids and the Nile and even rode a camel.

Maude had only a handful of close friends. She never married and didn't publicly acknowledge romantic interest in anyone, deliberately choosing her career over romance. "If Maude ever fell in love she probably wouldn't admit it to herself," her mother once told a reporter. "She is too occupied with her work to let her affections go too far." Maude didn't even like playing romantic parts and called her portrayal of Juliet a failure.

Unlike many stars of both her time and ours, she never sought publicity or revealed details of her private life. "The dominant motif of Maude Adams's life is minding her own business," one newspaper article about her began. The story ended with the idea that her very reticence in public made her the success she was onstage. Her private life was a mystery. She hid behind her work, avoiding social functions and refusing to give interviews to newspapers. They, of course, sometimes responded to her silence by publishing rumors and suppositions.

She preferred to spend time alone, reading books or making arrangements for the working farm she ran on Long Island, New York, which she bought in 1905. There, she built an estate where her mother could visit and where she could re-create the things she loved about her grandmother's farm in Utah.

Maude always recalled life in Salt Lake City fondly and continued to return. Her mother reluctantly retired in 1906 and moved back there. During a national tour, Maude was welcomed home with a celebration and was named "the state's most illustrious daughter."

In 1905 Barrie offered Maude a role she immediately knew would change her life. *Peter Pan* was a joyful celebration of the wonders of childhood, complete with pirates and crocodiles. But its language was poetic and lyrical. Maude's acting matched Barrie's writing—whimsical and yet unaffected, fresh and witty. The combination was perfect. Maude had played a boy before, in a production called *L'Aiglon* (a part she was said to do better than Sarah Bernhardt, one of the world's most storied actresses), and was ready to make her biggest departure from the world of tragedy.

The play renewed her flagging vigor and revived her spirit. "No actor lives by bread alone, and to have been part of that lovely play, to have known that wonderful feeling in an audience, is something to refresh one's spirit all of one's life, something to make one always grateful," she later wrote.

At first American audiences didn't know what to think of the Englishman's play, but they saw its magic once they began to bring their children to the theater. *Peter Pan* was one of the first plays families not only could but were expected to see together. Maude made sure ticket prices were low enough that anyone could afford them. And the experience was as much fun for the actors as it was for the audience.

Not only did the role open up a whole new world in the realm of acting, it finally gave her the chance to understand what it was like to be a child—something she had never really known, even in her own youth. The boy who refused to grow up transformed the woman who had never been a child. Finally, the "blank wall" between her and children came down, and she grew to love meeting her young fans.

She starred in *Peter Pan* from coast to coast and back again, enchanting both children and parents and making the character her own. Although some critics thought the play wasn't serious enough for someone of Maude's caliber, she got wild acclaim from fans of all ages, including Mark Twain, who wrote to Maude: "It is my belief that Peter

Pan is a great and refining and uplifting benefaction to this sordid and money-mad age; and that the next best play on the boards is a long way behind it as long as you play Peter."

The company revived the play several more times over the next decade or so. Maude went back to winning acclaim for more serious fare, including Barrie's *What Every Woman Knows.*

It was partly because of her frequent illness and exhaustion that she decided to retire from stage work in 1917. But she was suffering from great personal losses, too. Her mother, always her best friend, had died a year earlier; Maude had returned to Salt Lake City to be at her mother's bedside. Her grandmother had died only months before that. Just as devastating was the death of Charles Frohman, her good friend and mentor (they were also rumored to be lovers), in 1915 as a result of the sinking of the *Lusitania,* a British passenger ship torpedoed by German submarines during World War I.

Maude also wanted to focus on another aspect of her career: invention. Always interested in how stage lights worked, and intrigued by the new medium of film, she saw a need for better lighting and went to work with General Electric. At the time, lighting technology was quickly advancing, and the kerosene lamps of her childhood gave way to gas and finally electric lights, allowing for a greater range of possibilities onstage and in film. She devised lights that would be brighter but cooler.

She returned to the stage in 1929, and audiences looked forward to a great comeback. But Maude only took a few roles before she retired again for good. In the 1930s she did some work in radio, and her fans wondered if she might be willing to pursue film roles. David O. Selznick considered her for a part and went so far as to do a screen test, but Maude had little interest and didn't get the part.

Besides, she had just taken a post teaching drama at Stephens College in Missouri. In her new role she could pass her love of the theater on to a new generation, an idea she found more rewarding than anything else.

Maude retired from teaching in 1943 and died ten years later in New York. She was widely mourned and remembered. Even after her death she continued to draw attention. The female lead in the 1980 movie *Somewhere in Time,* starring Jane Seymour and Christopher Reeve, was based on her. And every time an actress (Peter is almost always played by a woman) takes on the role of the boy who never grew up, her performance is partly inspired by the way Maude Adams first brought him to life, more than a hundred years ago.

JOSIE AND ANN BASSETT

(1874–1964, 1878–1956)
WILD WEST SISTERS

Ann Bassett always loved to tell the story of the time Butch Cassidy's "Wild Bunch" held a Thanksgiving feast to thank the people of Brown's Park, a remote settlement on the Utah-Colorado border, for all the times the townsfolk had helped hide or provide for them. Butch, Elza Lay, and the rest of the outlaws put out a big spread that included rare winter delicacies: oysters, walnuts, tomatoes, and cheese.

Everyone dressed up for the fanciest event in Brown's Park history. The Bassett family loaned silver and china and linens for the occasion, and Ann and her sister Josie sat back to watch as the outlaws waited on their guests. Ann Bassett remembered later, telling the tale, that she wore a powder blue silk and taffeta dress and lace stockings. She presented a reading on the meaning of Thanksgiving, while her sister Josie played a tune on the zither.

Ann, who never lost a chance to make fun of someone, laughed at Butch as he served coffee. "Poor Butch, he could perform such minor jobs as robbing banks and holding up pay trains without a flicker of an eyelash, but serving coffee at a grand party, that was something else," she recalled years later.

"He became frustrated and embarrassed over the blunder he had made when some of the hosts told him it was not good form to pour coffee from a big black coffee pot and reach from left to right across the guests plate to grab a cup right under their noses," she went on. "The boys went into a huddle in the kitchen and instructed Butch in the more formal art of filling coffee cups at the table. This just shows how etiquette can put fear into a brave man's heart."

Ann Bassett went on trial for cattle rustling in 1911; from then on, folks called her "Queen of the Cattle Rustlers." Used by permission, Uintah County Library Regional History Center.

Having left her outlaw ways behind, Josie Bassett spent her later years tending her cabin and small farm. The cabin still stands today.

Ann and Josie could joke about the outlaws, because the boys were their friends.

The Bassett sisters not only helped them escape from authority but also rode along with them on the Outlaw Trail, the remote route Butch and others followed along the Green River from windswept Wyoming territory through eastern Utah to Arizona and New Mexico. The sisters were larger than life, hot tempered, and wily—as well as generous and resourceful. It's impossible to tell the story of one without the other.

The sisters grew up and lived much of their lives in Brown's Hole, the nickname for a verdant mountain-ringed valley on the Green River near the intersection of Utah, Colorado, and Wyoming. Even if lawmen had been interested in pursuing bandits into this place—which they rarely were—outlaws could just cross the border into the next jurisdiction to escape capture.

Far from any kind of settler authority, the area was still mostly occupied by Ute Indians and mountain men when the Bassett family arrived, one of several homesteading families who came to claim the 160 western acres the government gave any white settler willing to live on it. Their land was near the entrance to the valley, which made it a natural stopping point for travelers. Their homestead looked out over the foothills of surrounding mesas, the meandering river, a few stands of trees, and a sea of waving grass and brush.

Their father, Amos Herbert ("Herb") Bassett, was a musician and Civil War veteran who loved the finer things. His wife, Elizabeth, was the strong-willed, spirited daughter of a genteel Southern family. Looking for prosperity and a healthier environment for Herb, who had asthma, they moved west from their home in Arkansas. In 1877 they arrived at Brown's Hole. Herb's brother, Sam, was one of the valley's first permanent white residents, having gone west as one of the "mountain men" trapping and prospecting in the region.

Josie (given name Josephine) was four years old when the family made the move, and Elizabeth was pregnant with Ann. The girls would eventually have three brothers, one between them and two younger.

The Brown's Park citizenry, mostly male, were a colorful and diverse bunch that included permanent and temporary immigrants from Mexico, Australia, and Scotland as well as Ute Indians, whose people had lived in the area for generations. When Ann was born—the first white child born in Brown's Park—Elizabeth didn't have enough milk, and a Ute woman stepped in to nurse the baby.

The Bassett girls were a combination of their parents and their surroundings. Elizabeth Bassett decided Brown's Hole (which she preferred to call Brown's Park, its more civilized official name) was perfect for running cattle, and it was she who set up and ran the family's ranch. She helped build their house and herded the cows on horseback, later hiring and directing cowhands she won over with a magnetic personality and a willingness to jump in and work right alongside them.

Her employees included Isom Dart, a Black cowboy from Texas who would become a close family friend. The Bassett children worked alongside her as soon as they were old enough to ride horses.

Their well-respected, educated father was never very interested in the ranching business. Instead, he led church services and was appointed justice of the peace (where he sometimes had to turn a blind eye to the small-time cattle rustlers in the valley) and, later, the postmaster. He brought a diverse collection of books from back east and encouraged his daughters to read them. He also taught the local children during the winter. He loved to play the violin and hauled an organ from Arkansas so the girls could learn to play.

Their furnishings from the east were the best in the region, and their house, outfitted by Herb's craftsmanship, one of the nicest. The family entertained often, welcoming guests or travelers with dinner and a bed. Some of their guests were not quite law-abiding characters, and some family friends had connections to one of the bands of cattle rustlers moving through the area.

As they had elsewhere in the West, small-time ranchers tangled with the cattle barons who ran their livestock all over the region and sometimes onto homesteaders' ranges. Outlaws rustled the big spreads' cows, partly for food and money and partly out of spite. Banks and railroads—other big, faceless entities—would later become targets also.

In these small, far-flung settlements, day-to-day law enforcement didn't really exist. Outlaws, who often came from among the homesteaders' own communities, befriended the locals for protection and backup. Even the more law-abiding residents of Brown's Park were sometimes refugees from ugly situations, so they tended to be more sympathetic to the outlaws than those in a bigger town would have been.

Like their mother, Josie and Ann were comfortable around cowboys, whether they rustled on the side or not. Josie loved working the land and the household, and those who knew her saw her as a homebody. Ann was more hot-tempered and willful, and she liked to be outside running wild. Both girls were slender and attractive, with masses of curly warm brown hair. The sisters were always close, though their personalities were also very different. Throughout their lives they would fight often—yet they remained the closest of friends.

The Bassett family had enough money to send Josie and Ann to high school in Craig, Colorado, and Catholic boarding school in Salt Lake City. While Josie was a good student, unruly Ann was asked not to return after the first year. Instead, the family sent her to a school back east. She later would gleefully tell the story of what happened when the schoolmaster tried to teach her to ride like a lady. She jumped on the horse's back and took off. When the man tried to grab her bridle, she recalled, "I swung the horse about, with a prancing and rearing he had probably never before even attempted. Leaning from my saddle, I exclaimed vehemently, 'Go to hell, you repulsive little monkeyfaced skunk!'"

Ann was proud of her time at the boarding school, and even though she was always an outdoorswoman, she walked and talked and dressed like a sophisticated easterner.

Josie would never get a chance to graduate. Elizabeth Bassett died suddenly in 1892. Soon after, Josie married Jim McKnight, a longtime family friend and cowboy on the ranch. Four months later their son Crawford was born. The couple moved to their own land and had another son. Josie also helped her father run his homestead, cared for sick friends, and acted as the local midwife—not a big stretch considering the many calves she had delivered.

When Ann returned from school, she and Josie both helped out on the family ranch. One of their occasional companions was a young cowboy named Robert Leroy Parker, who had grown up in central Utah but left his Mormon family when he got into a scrape with the law. Parker—nickname Butch Cassidy—went from cowboy to small-time rustler to famous bank robber. He had a reputation for being not only good at his work but also friendly and generous. People knew him for a Robin Hood–style brand of justice and disinclination to violence; some said he visited poor families along the Outlaw Trail and brought them money or horses.

Some of the lawbreakers who sought refuge in the valley weren't as nice, and posses often rode through in pursuit of murderers. The Bassett ranch sometimes served as a base for the lawmen and stood in as a courthouse for informal proceedings against criminals. At least once, a man was dragged out and lynched by vigilantes there.

"Bob," as locals knew Butch Cassidy, worked on the Bassett ranch and others in his younger years, along with Matt Warner and Elza Lay, cowboys who would eventually become the core of the "Wild Bunch" gang of outlaws. Josie and Ann were two of a handful of adventurous girls who hung out with Wild Bunch men. Another was Maud Davis, who would end up marrying Elza. Outlaw gangs didn't usually allow women to travel with them, but these women were exceptional. They could keep up as the men rode hell for leather down the trail and would have no trouble enjoying stints in remote red-rock canyon hideouts.

Rumors swirled that Butch and Josie were romantically involved, but she would only ever call Butch a "good friend." Some have also floated the idea that Etta Place, Butch's most famous and mysterious girlfriend, was actually Ann Bassett. Ann and Butch definitely knew each other. Etta and Ann look similar in photos; both have smooth skin, pretty faces, and dark hair. And Ann did travel to some of the places where Butch was staying. But other times she definitely wasn't with him when Etta was said to be. And the Bassett sisters didn't tend to keep their relationships secret.

Besides, Ann apparently had another paramour: cowboy Matt Rash. In 1900 he was shot and killed in his own cabin at Brown's Park, probably a victim of the cattle wars raging between small and large ranchers. He was a high-profile target because he had been working to keep herds separate. When he died his will disappeared, but Ann must have thought she was his beneficiary. She filed a lawsuit asking to have his estate go through probate (she withdrew the suit after she and his family came to an arrangement in which she got $250).

By this time Butch and his gang were more often than not using Robbers Roost, a remote canyon in the southeastern Utah desert, as their base of operations. Few women would have been inclined to ride the narrow Green River canyons and set up camp in the desert on the southern end of the Outlaw Trail. That wouldn't have deterred the Bassett sisters.

While Butch Cassidy, Etta Place, and Harry Longabaugh—the Sundance Kid—fled to Argentina in 1904, Elza Lay returned and worked again as a rancher in Brown's Park. Soon after, Butch and Sundance were killed by a posse in South America. Or were they? Ann was one of several people who reported seeing Butch in America again, years later. But if Ann was indeed Etta Place, she didn't tell anyone about her trip to South America.

In the meantime Josie was happy working the land and taking care of the children, but she soon butted heads with her husband. When he wanted to move to Vernal and open a saloon, she refused to leave their ranch, which was in her name. She filed for divorce and custody of their two sons, but he took the children, a move that would spark one of the more notorious events in Josie's life. Josie asked Jim to come to where she was staying in Colorado to negotiate a truce; when he arrived, Josie was surrounded by friends (including Ann) who were angry at him on her behalf.

When they tried to serve him with papers, Jim turned and ran. A deputy sheriff chased after him and shot him in the back, a glancing blow that knocked him down. Though the wound was not serious and Josie and Jim ultimately divorced amicably, the incident became part of Bassett legend. As the story went around, it morphed into Josie herself shooting her husband. She would later brush off the idea: "No, I didn't shoot him," she said. "If I had, I wouldn't have missed!"

Josie's father convinced her that a remote cattle ranch wasn't a good place for her to raise her children alone. Though she certainly could have run the ranch, she wanted to give her boys an education, so she reluctantly sold her 680 cattle, moved to Craig, Colorado, and found work running a hotel. She made a living, but it never made her happy.

That year was a difficult one for the whole family. Herb Bassett, who had never enjoyed frontier life, decided to travel the country meeting fellow veterans and staying in various retirement homes for Union soldiers. That left Ann and her brothers Eb and George in charge of the Brown's Park homestead.

Then, the family's old friend Isom Dart was shot and killed while working with George, the youngest Bassett brother. Ann wasn't happy with the authorities' failure to find his murderer. Like many in Brown's Park, she blamed the big cattle ranchers, who sent their own enforcers (a private detective named Tom Horn, in particular) to harass local ranchers they knew were sympathetic to rustlers. Later that fall Ann showed newspapers around Colorado a letter warning her to leave the area in thirty days or be killed.

Not only did Ann refuse to leave, she was furious, and she waged a war against the big ranchers in the only way she knew how. When the barons' cattle came into what she considered her territory, she ran them into the Green River, where they were either killed or swept downstream to become someone else's problem. Her reputation as a rustler grew.

Josie was again fighting her own battles. In 1902 she married Charley Ranney, a pharmacist in Craig. She was looking for stability and a way out of the boardinghouse business. He was a respected man, but he wasn't exciting enough for her (or for her younger son, Chick, who soon started spending much of his time at his aunt Ann's ranch). That marriage only lasted four years, until Josie left him for another man. Her third marriage was even more short-lived—within six months the man was gone.

She worked in boardinghouses until her sons were out of school. In 1911 she returned again to Brown's Park with her fourth husband, Emerson "Nig" Wells. He was a nice guy—when he wasn't drinking, which wasn't very often. Only two years later he died after a three-day drinking binge in Wyoming. Rumors started to swirl that she had poisoned him after an argument. In reality he probably either drank himself to death or had a bad reaction to one of the "cures" for alcoholism that were popular at the time. Whatever the cause, his death added to her legend, which like Ann's was based on a mixture of truth and tall tales.

Ann had her own small ranch but wanted a bigger spread. She also knew her own power over men. She combined the two by marrying Hi Bernard, foreman on one of the most successful cattle ranches in western Colorado—the same one that had employed Tom Horn, her former flame's suspected murderer. This was a case of "if you can't beat 'em, join 'em." She combined her assets with his and went to work herding cattle.

By 1910 Hi was tired of playing second fiddle to his strong-willed wife, and he left for Denver. As battles raged over control of the open range, Ann continued her campaign against the big operators, going so far as to rustle some of their cattle for herself. She had long been rumored to do this on a small scale. But they didn't press charges until she closed off her watering hole to their cattle.

Ann went on trial in Craig in the summer of 1911. The townsfolk packed the proceedings, which ended in a mistrial. The second trial dragged on for two years and ended in dramatic fashion when one of

Ann's defense lawyers asked her nemesis Ora Haley, the owner of the largest herd around, how many cattle he had. It turned out that the number he named was a lot larger than the number he had claimed when he paid his taxes. His credibility was destroyed, Ann was acquitted, and her supporters spent the night drinking, celebrating, and firing their pistols into the air. Ann treated everyone in town to dinner and a movie.

"Queen" Ann (as she was known after her trial, when she was called "Queen of the Cattle Rustlers") soon staked a claim a few miles away from where Josie had finally followed her dream and carved out a remote homestead on Cub Creek near Jensen, Utah, a few miles southwest of Brown's Park. Josie had assistance from Ben Morris, a rough cowboy who had worked for her before and whom she married by the end of 1913. She needed his financial and physical help in setting up the homestead. She planted fruit trees and a garden, moved her animals to the land, and planned her future, hoping to one day run a guest ranch as well as a working one.

Ann was less interested in becoming a legitimate businesswoman and instead used her cabin as a way station for her outlaw friends moving up and down the trail. In return they gave her a share of their proceeds. Ann also spent much of her time visiting friends or relatives. Unlike Josie, she couldn't be satisfied with work-filled days in the middle of nowhere.

In 1923 Ann married her own cowboy, longtime friend Frank Willis. She was thirty-six and ready to settle down a little. Their relationship was happy, with only an occasional quick spat. Somehow, the more quarrelsome of the sisters ended up with the best marriage.

Josie once again grew tired of her husband, and after one last argument, she chased Ben Morris out of the house for good. Someone asked him why he was so far from home and he said, "Well, she gave me three minutes to leave and I've got two of them left and I've been riding in circles ever since." Josie remained friends with Ben, just as she had with her other husbands. She had a temper but didn't hold grudges.

By the time her son Crawford and his wife returned after World War I, Josie was spending much of her time with Ed Lewis, the cowboy who owned the neighboring homestead—a relationship that also eventually fizzled. As one magazine writer tactfully put it in a retrospective on Josie's life: "It requires more delicate language than the writer can presently muster to describe Josie's romances."

Josie had the ranch running well enough that she didn't need a man around, anyway. Though Crawford often came over to help out, she did much of the work herself. She chopped wood, caught her own fish, and hunted her own deer (it was said she always got her buck, even when it wasn't hunting season). As one observer noted in her day, "It is said of Josie that she can kill a beef on the range, skin it out, dress it, and have it hanging up in forty-five minutes. This is a challenge to the most dexterous men."

Josie built a new cabin for herself in the 1930s. She took advantage of her solitude and started up a thriving bootlegging business during Prohibition, supplementing her and Crawford's income with whiskey and sweet wines, though she and Ann almost never drank.

Almost everyone who knew Josie respected and admired her. On the other hand, she was known as a good shot who wouldn't take any nonsense. During the Depression, when Josie was sixty-two, one of her neighbors accused her of rustling some of his cattle, skinning them, and selling the meat (no one minded when she took the occasional stray cow for herself or needy friends, but to sell the meat was going too far). The trial resulted in two hung juries—jurors just couldn't bring themselves to decide against this very pleasant gray-haired lady.

Her home was always open to travelers or anyone who needed help. She and Ann were both known for their generosity, even when it wasn't quite legal. They gave meat from "stray" cows to their down-on-their-luck neighbors. Their neighbors, who knew the sisters' history, were both proud and scandalized.

Ann and Frank moved to California, Nevada, and Arizona, where Ann helped Frank and Josie's son Chick (who had worked for a time as a movie cowboy) run cattle and sheep ranches. In 1944 she moved back to the family homestead at Brown's Park and built her own cabin there. She spent winters in Leeds, Utah, an old mining town north of St. George.

By the time they were middle-aged, the two sisters had been through seven husbands, several homesteads, shootings, legal troubles, and family heartache. Josie would never have the big ranch she wanted, but she was happy running her small farm, where her grandchildren and Ann and Frank came to work and play every summer.

Stories about these colorful women started circulating almost as they happened, and as they got older, people continued to be interested in hearing about their lives. A couple of early books about Brown's Park portrayed it as a wild place full of thieves and gangsters, which wasn't the way Ann and Josie remembered it. While it had its share of shady characters (including them), they always saw it as a neighborly and civilized place. Ann wrote some of her memoirs, and there was talk off and on about a movie based on them. They would have welcomed that, since it would have helped them financially and refuted some of the nastier stories about them. But it never happened.

Life magazine did come by and do a story, mostly about the independent Josie, in the 1940s. The magazine featured her dressing a deer and making it into dinner for assembled friends. A couple of years later, Josie was invited to be an honorary rodeo queen in Vernal. Delighted but a bit embarrassed, she accepted and had a great time showing off in her best duds. She also won third place in a horse race. She was almost eighty.

By then both sisters had long given up wearing skirts. Josie's skin was wrinkled and mottled with age, while Ann (who had always used creams and worn a hat to shade her face) looked relatively youthful. But Ann, the younger sister, would die first. In 1956 she succumbed to heart disease. Before she died she insisted that her ashes be spread in Brown's Park, but her grieving husband famously carried them around in the trunk of his car until he died in 1963. The family quietly buried them near their homestead.

Josie remained in her cabin, gardening, keeping a few animals, and riding her horse. She was alone but not lonely—she continued to take in travelers and welcome visitors (by this time, she was something of a tourist attraction). She died in 1964 and was buried next to her mother and sister in Brown's Park.

Josie's cabin still stands, now weathered and surrounded by overgrown gardens, preserved as part of Dinosaur National Monument. It's a good bet most visitors would better appreciate its significance if they knew the rollicking story of the Bassetts.

REVA BECK BOSONE

(1895–1983)

LAWYER, JUDGE, CONGRESSWOMAN

Reva Beck Bosone had her first memorable run-in with authority when she ran for student body president in high school. As election day drew nearer, she was on track to become the first girl in state history to win that office.

Then one day the school principal called her into his office and suggested she run for vice president instead. It just didn't seem right for a girl to win, he said. Bowing to his wishes, she dropped out of the race for president and agreed to be vice president. As something of a consolation prize, she was selected the town's "Goddess of Liberty" later that year—something the principal no doubt thought was more suitable.

That was the last time Reva would ever let someone convince her to hold back based on her gender. From then on, if there was an office she wanted, she would run for it. And chances were that she would win. One of Utah's most successful politicians, she served two terms in the state legislature, twelve years as the state's first woman judge, and two terms in the U.S. House of Representatives.

Reva Zilpha Beck was born in 1895 to Christian M. Beck and Zilpha Chipman Beck. They were descended from some of Utah's earliest Mormon arrivals, but the family had left the church over polygamy. Reva was a fighter—and a handful—from the start. In her unpublished memoirs, she wrote: "A thirteen-pound baby is enough to kill any mother. Part of my thirteen pounds at birth must have been a wrought-iron jaw. Otherwise I would have been knocked out of politics long ago."

Although it wasn't common for women to become lawyers in her day, law was in her DNA. The Beck family held to a saying: "If you want

Reva Beck Bosone was one of Utah's most successful politicians. It's a good bet she's voting for herself in this election.

to do good, go where the laws are made." She and two of her three brothers would practice law, and one of her brothers also became a judge.

Reva grew up in American Fork, a medium-sized town between Salt Lake City and Provo, where her family owned the town's best hotel. At first, her body was not quite as strong as her intellect. She had a heart condition and was kept out of any strenuous activity until she was a teenager. But there was plenty at home to keep her mind occupied.

The family loved debating over government and current affairs. Reva was the only girl, but she could hold her own. She later credited those many discussions with not only igniting her passion for making a difference in the world but also for giving her a lot of practice at getting along with men.

Reva's parents eventually made enough money to buy the town's opera house, where she acted in local productions. Tall, with green eyes and red hair, she thought about making a living on the stage. "It was decided long before I was grown up that I would graduate from college, then go to New York City and attend a dramatic art school," she later recalled. But her mother talked her out of becoming a professional actor, and Reva lost interest.

Her vibrant personality didn't come naturally at first. As a student, she was inclined to be shy and self-conscious. She was keenly aware of her above-average height and red hair, which she thought made her stand out a little too much. But by the time she was in high school, with her family's encouragement, she had worked to overcome her insecurities and built an armor of competence around herself that she would later use to brush off criticism.

She was a good student, with a special talent when it came to memorizing information and reciting it later. Not surprisingly, she was on her high school debate team.

She always knew she would go to college. She attended Westminster College in Salt Lake City, then a two-year school, and graduated in 1917.

While her brothers went off for further study at the University of Utah, Reva headed for the University of California at Berkeley, where her mother had always wanted one of her children to study. Reva studied English and graduated in 1919 after having won the admiration of her teachers and peers—and survived a severe bout of influenza during the epidemic of 1918.

Although she knew she wanted to become a lawyer, one of her brothers suggested she might want to wait until she was a bit older. It would be hard enough for a woman to be taken seriously as a lawyer, but it might be impossible for a young one. She returned to American Fork to live at home, work as a teacher for a few years, and save up for law school.

At twenty-five she married Harold G. Cutler, but it wasn't a good match, and they were divorced within a year. Over the next few years, she moved through a series of jobs that each paid a little better and gave her more of the freedom and authority she wanted. She taught in the eastern Utah town of Delta before moving to Ogden.

At the time, Ogden was the state's second-largest city, a thriving railroad town with cultural aspirations that matched Reva's. She taught English, speech, drama, and debate, becoming the head of Ogden High School's speech and drama department. She directed school plays and coached the debate team.

What could have been a fallback career flourished into a passion, and everyone at school loved Reva. Her magnetic personality and engaging speaking style urged students to work harder even as they were having fun. After school "Miss Beck" became "Reva," as students hung around her classroom to tell her stories and ask her advice on subjects they didn't dare discuss with their parents.

Reva's life outside school activities was as austere as her professional life was crowded. She wore only two dresses, both simple and black (she wore one while the other got cleaned), and while her colleagues spent their summers traveling, she returned home to help clean the family hotel. By 1926 she had saved enough to take the big trip she had always wanted: a three-month, nine-country tour of Europe.

She returned happy but exhausted, only to get into a dispute with the school superintendent over her salary. He told her that although her performance was as good as ever, he couldn't keep giving her the same raises he had been. The event was a catalyst that steered her back to her original plan. She resigned and signed up for law school at the University of Utah, where she was one of two women in her law school class and the only one who graduated.

Years later, when she was making a speech, she saw the superintendent in the audience. "I introduced him as a man who had done me a tremendous favor. He really beamed," she recalled. "And then I proceeded to relate the event that had hastened my study of law—much to his discomfiture, I believe."

Some people were mystified at why a woman would want to give up a successful teaching career to go back to school. But for Reva, it was a logical next step. She wanted to be a lawyer for the same reason she did almost everything in her life: to make a difference in the world. And she decided the best way to do that was to get into politics. She knew law was a traditional route to becoming a legislator. That, on top of the chance to help average people fight their legal battles, made her decision.

She would never entirely give up teaching, nor her view of herself as a teacher. During law school she taught a freshman English class and was so popular that during one term, fifty students signed up for her class—and that was far too many. The department asked for ten volunteers to drop the class and got no takers, no matter how much she or the department chair begged. "Way down deep, I glowed!" Reva wrote in her memoirs. "Does anyone wonder why I'd like to wind up my life teaching?"

During law school she also met Joseph Bosone, a fellow student. He was a devout Catholic, but she didn't want her children raised in a strict

Italian Catholic household. They tried to break up, but they couldn't bear being apart. When they got back together, he took her to meet his parents in the small town of Helper, near Price in eastern Utah. In this rough-and-tumble mining town at the base of yellow, coal-filled cliffs, she fell in love with his family and their close-knit immigrant community. The couple quietly married in 1929.

In 1930 Reva's oldest brother, Clarence, made the motion to admit her to the bar; she was the eleventh woman in the state to be accepted. She decided to practice law under her maiden name as a sign of her independence but eventually added her married name, partly to placate her hurt mother-in-law.

Reva practiced law with her brother, then took time off to have a baby daughter she named Zilpha after her mother. But Reva was soon back at work, though she stayed in Helper so Joe's mother could watch the baby while he and Reva practiced law. Reva wasn't sure the diverse populace in this mining region would accept her, but she quickly made herself a visible figure on the local scene.

She didn't back down from challenges. As a lawyer who worked in a somewhat gritty mining town and was sympathetic to the working class, she represented some unsavory clients, including a couple of sex workers. In one of her first cases, she defended two boys accused of rape in a highly publicized trial and won the case after pointing out holes in the accusers' stories. Her victory broke the prosecutor's two-year winning streak.

In 1932, less than two years after moving to Helper, she ran for the state legislature. Her desire to help working-class people led her to become a Democrat, though she grew up in a family of Republicans. She canvassed door-to-door to introduce herself, sometimes with her two-year-old daughter in tow, impressing the people she met with her self-assured but unassuming manner. She won as part of a statewide Democratic landslide and was one of six female legislators heading to the state capitol in 1933.

It was the height of the Great Depression, and everyone was concerned about economic and labor issues. Reva was chosen to be a member of eight committees in the state legislature and focused on labor laws dealing with minimum wage and child labor.

Hoping to make a better living from their practice, Reva and Joe moved to Salt Lake City, where they continued to take all kinds of cases. Since she was no longer a resident of Carbon County, she resigned from her seat in the legislature. Even though she had just moved to a new and much bigger city, she was confident she would be elected again from her new district—and she was.

She ran for speaker of the state house of representatives; though she lost that by a few votes, she was chosen as the House Democratic majority leader.

In 1936 a distinguished judge encouraged her to run for the office herself. Never one to back down from a challenge or a good idea, Reva agreed. She won, and was elected Utah's first female judge. In Salt Lake City's Police and Traffic court, she heard all kinds of cases. She was known as fair and unflappable, although she was nervous at first, knowing a spotlight was on her.

She was known for impatience with bad drivers and raised the fines for drunken and reckless driving to deter offenders. Tired of levying so many fines and hearing so many stories about bad drivers, she instituted the state's first traffic school. (Once, a *Deseret News* reporter offered to get rid of any unflattering photos of her that the newspaper had on file if she would dismiss his traffic ticket. She declined the offer and said he was lucky to get away with just his fine.)

She also had a weekly radio show, where she talked in general about her experiences and warned people about the consequences of breaking the law.

She tried to treat everyone fairly, from well-known figures to the prostitutes, drunks, and hardscrabble thieves who showed up in her court. She was one of the first judges to order psychiatric evaluations of defendants, in case extenuating circumstances could help her make a better decision. She looked for ways to rehabilitate those who could be helped, and she was one of the first judges in Utah to send people with drinking problems to Alcoholics Anonymous. She helped found the Utah State Board for Education on Alcoholism and accepted a position as its chairwoman, approaching alcoholism as a disease and education as one of its cures.

The office had a fun side, too. The first marriage ceremony she presided over, at the elegant Hotel Utah, joined starlet Marla Shelton and Jack Dawn, an MGM makeup man. They later divorced.

Reva's own marriage hit rocky times by 1940, when she found evidence that Joe was having affairs. She was heartbroken, but she couldn't go along with his pleas to stay together. Always a woman of principle, she asked for a divorce.

Reva kept busy as a member of several political, social, and business organizations. She also recruited for the Women's Army Corps, which helped on the "home front" during World War II. After the war she was an official observer at the founding of the United Nations and helped write a women's equality clause for its charter.

Through the 1940s Reva's associates urged her to run for national office. She joined the U.S. House race in 1948 and campaigned with Harry Truman. Even she was pretty sure she wouldn't make it—after all, she was not only a woman but a single parent, and she was running against an incumbent, William A. Dawson. She also wasn't Mormon. To many people's surprise, both she and Truman won.

Reva and Zilpha, by this time a college student but always close to her mother, moved together to Washington and explored the new city. Zilpha always agreed with her mother that gender shouldn't be an impediment, and a couple of years later she joined the Air Force (Reva spoke at her graduation). She went on to be the first woman intelligence officer ever for an American Air Force squadron.

Reva wanted to be on the Interior Committee, an important one for Utah since it deals with land use and natural resources. When she inquired about the possibility, she heard back that no woman had ever been on it and no woman should—because the committee might at some point have to discuss "animal breeding." A bemused Reva responded that after hearing so much as a judge about human sex, animal breeding would be nothing. She won the appointment . . . and never heard a discussion of animal breeding. She used her post on the committee as a springboard to help resolve water and soil conservation issues in the West.

As she had everywhere, she made many friends in Washington and was known for being a conscientious and principled legislator. She also used her speaking skills to her advantage. Early in her tenure, she was invited to speak at the Women's National Press Club Dinner. She didn't know she would be asked to speak first, and she walked to the stage not knowing what she was going to say. She saved herself by doing an impersonation of the many men who had appeared before her while still drunk. "Jedge, you here again?" she slurred. It was a memorable performance that made her some immediate friends who would come in handy later.

She continued to feel she shouldn't be treated any differently because she was a woman. A vote in Congress was worth the same whether cast by a man or a woman, was it not?

Once, the U.S. Navy invited members of Congress to spend a weekend aboard a naval carrier. She happily accepted—but the Navy withdrew its invitation when it learned she was a woman. The ship, it said, didn't have "facilities" for women.

Reva argued that since any family's "facilities" are used by all members of the family, that shouldn't be a problem. Not only did they let her, another congresswoman, and a female reporter go on the trip, they let the women sleep in the admiral's quarters.

For the 1950 campaign, the Republicans chose a woman, Ivy Baker Priest, to run against Reva (Priest would later become the U.S. Treasurer). The women respected each other too much to fight a dirty campaign, though Priest attacked Reva for her efforts to reform the health-care system. The "socialized medicine" charge didn't work, and Reva was reelected.

Things were more difficult the next time around. In 1952, in the middle of the McCarthyist anti-communism crusade, Reva's opponents called her a communist. That was partly based on Reva's opposition to a bill that made it illegal for the federal government to hire anyone with communist sympathies. She had also voted against the creation of the CIA. She thought those measures threatened civil liberties and could hurt innocent people, and she didn't like the idea of the government covertly keeping tabs on its citizens.

William Dawson, trying to retake the seat Reva won in 1948, not only brought up the "socialized medicine" charge but also said she had engaged in "unladylike conduct" and reminded voters that she was divorced. The most damning charge, considering the time and place, implied Reva was a communist. One piece of campaign literature proclaimed, "You, Reva Beck Bosone, have sold your heritage to the Kremlin."

Dawson won, part of a wave of Republicans swept in during the Eisenhower years. The campaign wounded Reva deeply, and Dawson was the only opponent she was never interested in befriending. Utah wouldn't get its next female congresswoman until Karen Shepherd won in 1992.

Reva returned to Salt Lake City and busied herself with a new television show discussing current events. Afraid she might run for Congress again in the next election, her political opponents called her advertisers to complain.

Reva did run in 1954, and this time the race was dirtier than ever, with opponents spreading rumors that she was a drunk (a strange charge, considering her career—and the fact that she rarely drank). She felt her opponents were trying to swing women voters against her by attacking her character even as they took advantage of national hysteria over the communist threat. At the same time, the old "New Deal" Democratic party was losing its appeal in Utah, where voters were turning more conservative in general.

She lost the election. More devastating, she was treated as something of a pariah in Utah's political circles, and for a while she had a hard time finding another job.

She decided to go back to Washington, where she was hired as legal counsel for a congressional subcommittee on education in 1958. In 1961 she took a job as the highest-ranking judicial officer in the U.S. Post Office—which required her to look into everything from fraud to obscenity.

She retired in 1968, spending her time traveling, visiting friends, writing many letters, giving advice, and accepting awards. Those included an honorary Ph.D. from the University of Utah and the UC Berkeley Distinguished Service in Government Award in 1970. Irving Stone included her among thirty-nine distinguished alumni in the history he compiled of UC Berkeley. Reva died in Virginia in 1983.

When Reva Beck Bosone retired from her postal service job, the *Salt Lake Tribune* wrote, "Retirement is a difficult step to take when the person involved is being nagged by apprehensions of things being left uncompleted. Fortunately for Reva Beck Bosone, who leaves public office Saturday after 40 years of service, there need be no such anxiety." That was an apt summary of a life spent making a difference for other people—which is exactly what Reva set out to do.

JUANITA BROOKS

(1898–1989)
HISTORIAN WHO SOUGHT THE TRUTH

When Juanita Brooks first stood on a hill and looked out over the valley called Mountain Meadows, she pondered what she knew about this mysterious place—and what she didn't.

She grew up hearing that many years earlier, this quiet place was the site of a horrific massacre. She had been told that Indians had raided a convoy of white immigrants and slaughtered most of them. But she and others were starting to suspect the place held dark secrets that implicated some of her neighbors' ancestors. Overlooking the slopes around Mountain Meadows and into the vast Great Basin desert beyond, the young schoolteacher had a feeling many of those who committed the crime were never held accountable.

In her memoirs she recalled the moment the thought struck her. "Men did not gather here by chance or mere hearsay. If they were here, they had come because they were ordered to come. And whatever went on was done because it had been ordered, not because individuals had acted upon impulse."

Moments like this convinced her she must find the truth about Mountain Meadows and tell it to the world.

Juanita Brooks was driven by a desire to find and tell truths about history, and she was determined to bring a clear-eyed perspective to it. Although she lived her whole life as a faithful Mormon, she wrote about the church's warts as well as its positives. She was one of the first Utah historians to take a critical look at her homeland's history—an aim that didn't endear her to those who preferred that the past be left sleeping.

Juanita Brooks was a beloved scholar and historian, though she risked a backlash when she started investigating the Mountain Meadows Massacre. Used by permission, Utah State Historical Society. All rights reserved.

She was already well known as a historian and a teacher when she tackled the Mountain Meadows Massacre, one of the most controversial subjects in Mormon history. But as much as a historian, she was a biographer, seeking to humanize history and tell the life stories of regular people.

Juanita Leone Leavitt was born in 1898 in Bunkerville, Nevada, a desert Mormon settlement just southwest of the Utah border. She got her effervescent energy from her mother, who did much of the work on their small homestead, which was surrounded by jagged mountain ranges, high mesas, and miles of vast, open desert. As the oldest child, she helped her father with his mail route, capturing fresh horses to bring to him. The family also rented out half of the house to the local school, which gave Juanita a chance to listen in on lessons before she was old enough to attend.

She was always a little self-conscious about her appearance—thin, with a large nose and crooked teeth (her teeth only got worse until she finally got dentures decades later). Juanita was an excellent student and skipped first grade but was held back in the sixth because she looked so sickly the teacher refused to accept her in his class. As an adult, she tended to keep her hair pulled back and wore practical clothes. She overcame lifelong insecurities about her appearance with a gregarious personality and witty conversation.

After graduating from high school and spending a year helping out at her cousins' farm, she went to a nearby "normal school" to become a teacher. Her teacher, a Columbia University graduate, inspired Juanita and opened her eyes to the way people outside Mormonism viewed the world.

After graduating she taught at the elementary school in Bunkerville, then in nearby Mesquite. While she was working as a teacher, she got to know many of the residents and earned their respect.

One of those she befriended was the local patriarch, an elderly man tasked with giving special blessings to young church members. One day the old man asked her to help him write something important, but she was busy and put him off. Shortly thereafter, she heard that he was calling for her from his deathbed. By the time she got to him, he was too far gone.

As she recalled in her memoirs: "He seemed troubled; he rambled in delirium—he prayed, he yelled, he preached, and once his eyes opened wide to the ceiling and he yelled, 'BLOOD! BLOOD! BLOOD!'"

Juanita was alarmed. "What is the matter with him?" she asked a relative. "He acts like he is haunted."

"Maybe he is," the man replied. "He was at the Mountain Meadows Massacre, you know."

Juanita was shocked. She blasted herself for not immediately grabbing a chance to hear a firsthand account of the massacre that happened sixty years before. It was the first time she began asking questions about the event that would become a major focus in her life.

She married Ernest Pulsipher at age twenty-one, but he died of cancer soon afterward, leaving her and a baby son. With dreams of higher education, she helped work her in-laws' farm and took odd jobs to save money for college. She graduated from Brigham Young University in Provo after excelling as a debater and taking summer courses in writing. She took classes in everything from economics to English to education, but her degree was in food and nutrition because those were the classes she could take while neighbors and housemates watched her son.

She moved to St. George in southwestern Utah to teach English, public speaking, and debate at Dixie College. St. George was like an oasis in the desert, a cultural center near where she grew up. It was far from any major city: Salt Lake City was 300 miles away, Las Vegas was then little more than a rest stop in the desert, and Los Angeles was nearly 400 miles distant. It was founded when Brigham Young sent settlers to the Southwest, hoping they could grow cotton and other warm-weather crops (thus the nickname "Dixie").

In 1928 Juanita used a paid sabbatical to make the long trip to New York City, where, inspired by her former teacher, she earned a master's degree at Columbia University. It was a big challenge, at a time when women—and especially single mothers—weren't expected to try for such things. Jumping into a thesis about American literature gave her invaluable experience in doing in-depth research, and living in a cosmopolitan eastern city gave her a whole new perspective on the world outside of Utah and Mormonism.

She returned to St. George, where she was appointed dean of women at Dixie College. She had a huge impact on the sleepy town, helping it mature into an independent city with its own cultural assets. Long before she was nationally famous, she was a powerful force for historical preservation and documentation. She wanted to tell the history of "Utah's Dixie," which wasn't well known to those outside the region.

Like other Mormons who settled the West, the settlers here kept detailed diaries. Few outsiders could make much of an inroads into the region's collective psyche, but Juanita could. During her long and busy career, the region would give her plenty of untapped history to mine—and her status as a local helped her win the trust of those who had the information she needed.

The LDS Church founded the college that later became Dixie State in 1911. By 1933, when Juanita left to raise children with her second husband, it had become an official state college. She would return again several times, spending much of her adult life as a teacher there. She was known as a hard grader and rarely gave A's. She could both inspire students with wry, funny stories and terrify them with red-ink comments on their essays.

In 1931 she had her first long conversation with Will Brooks, a local sheriff (he later worked as the regional postmaster) as he was giving her a ride to the other side of southern Utah. After his wife died in 1932, he courted her, and they were married in 1933. He was seventeen years her senior and had four sons.

Although Juanita loved her professional life, she was ready to move beyond being everyone's favorite sister, aunt, or cousin and become a full-fledged wife. She felt responsible for making the merged household work, and she loved family more than anything else—and very quickly, she discovered she was pregnant. She and Will would go on to have four more children over the next five years, adding to their already boisterous family.

Juanita was also called by the church to be the regional president for the Relief Society, a demanding job in itself that required organizing everything from big ceremonies to visits with local congregations she supervised.

She had always loved and doted on everyone in her family, giving help and serving as a second mother to her younger siblings. She handled her home life with the enthusiasm she applied to everything. She was a multitasker, always keeping ironing handy in case guests dropped by so she could have something to do while they conversed.

There was no time for major academic pursuits. Instead, Juanita focused her intellect on writing freelance articles. She earned a reputation for approaching her historical accounts of southern Utah in a balanced, thoroughly researched yet entertaining way. One of her first articles, about polygamy, was published in *Harper's Magazine*. It was a major triumph that got people talking.

Most readers, including many who had never heard of Juanita Brooks, thought she did an admirable job with a tough subject. One elderly polygamist wrote to her: "The theme is a delicate one for some of us, and such abhorrence for others of us, that to discuss it frankly and freely and to do it with a grace and such supreme good-taste that no one can fail to be pleased is a real achievement."

She began traveling throughout the state and the West speaking, lecturing, serving on panels, and helping other scholars with their research—activities she would squeeze into her schedule throughout her life. She was well regarded enough to write for both the *Salt Lake*

Tribune, which had never befriended Mormons, and the Relief Society's official magazine.

She took charge of several major projects for the Utah State Historical Society, for which she was assistant state supervisor. During the Great Depression she oversaw collection and transcription of diaries and oral histories under the Works Progress Administration. She reserved space in a back room of her house where women came in to type the reminiscences of their forebears, copies of which eventually made it into the Library of Congress's collection in Washington, D.C.

As Relief Society president, Juanita had access to historical documents stored in the St. George temple; only church officials had full access to the sacred building. She pored over them, developing an even deeper knowledge of the people who had settled the region over the previous few decades. Never one to get much sleep, she often stayed up late to make typed copies of their diaries.

After writing a few more history-oriented articles for regional and national magazines, Juanita wanted to pursue a bigger project. Writers were starting to use scholarly tools to reexamine Mormon history, sometimes causing controversy in the process. They included Fawn Brodie, a church member whose *No Man Knows My History* delved into the life of the church's founder, Joseph Smith. When she portrayed him as a charming opportunist, the church excommunicated her.

Juanita wanted to write a book about frontiersman Jacob Hamblin, one of St. George's most important founders. While researching the Hamblin book, she took some time out to write a biography of her grandfather, Dudley Leavitt, a hearty pioneer who had forty-eight children by five wives and who became the forebear of a significant segment of southern Utah's population.

During her research she soon realized Jacob Hamblin had somehow been involved in the Mountain Meadows Massacre—a subject no one in southern Utah wanted to talk about.

St. George's early years were marked not only by the usual pioneer hardships but by an event that historian and Juanita Brooks biographer Levi S. Peterson says caused "a guilt as devastating and ineradicable as that which afflicted the participants in the Salem witch trials in the late seventeenth century": the Mountain Meadows Massacre.

At the time of the massacre, the U.S. government was growing increasingly suspicious of Mormons—and vice versa. As distrust grew, the federal government sent troops to keep an eye on the Mormons and remind them that they were still subject to U.S. authority. Mormons feared that war would erupt at any moment and they would have nowhere to go. They mustered a statewide militia that stood ready to fight the Army if necessary.

Mountain Meadows is a high-elevation mountain valley north of St. George where immigrants en route to California watered and rested their convoys before the trip across the bone-dry desert. In 1857 a group of about 120 immigrants passing through from Arkansas to California, the Fancher party, were attacked by a group of Paiute Indians, who killed all the men and women and most of the children.

Shortly before the massacre, members of the Fancher party had circled their wagons and defended themselves during a five-day initial siege by the Paiutes, during which several immigrants were killed.

A short time later, militia leader John D. Lee went to Mountain Meadows and offered the Fancher group peaceful passage. When the immigrants uncircled their wagons, the Indians killed everyone old enough to identify them, took the youngest children with them, and left the bodies scattered all over the hillsides. Local Mormons took in the surviving children to raise as their own.

That was the original story. But details emerged after the event, and it grew clear to Juanita and others that someone had recruited the Indians to attack the immigrants.

For one thing, the travelers known as the Fancher party had clashed with Mormon settlers in the area before the massacre. The Fancher party had asked the Mormons to sell them food; the Mormons refused. Mormons were still upset over the way they had been treated in Missouri twenty years earlier, before the flight to Utah. Some members of the Fancher party were from Missouri—and personally opposed to Mormonism. The rest of the group was from Arkansas. As Mormons geared up for a possible war with the U.S. government, Mormon apostle Parley P. Pratt was killed in Arkansas by a man whose wife had left him to join the Mormons and become one of Pratt's wives.

After the Civil War, federal investigators looked into the massacre and indicted nine men but convicted only John D. Lee, who was hanged in 1877. When Juanita interviewed descendants of Jacob Hamblin, a local Mormon leader at the time of the massacre, they still reacted angrily to any mention of Lee. Lee's descendants reacted the same way to mentions of Hamblin, whom they saw as one of many who used their ancestor as a scapegoat. It seemed everyone was trying to paint the other side's forebear as villain and theirs as hero.

In the years following the massacre, bits and pieces of the story had trickled out (Ann Eliza Webb Young had written about it in her memoir, for example), but no one had done a thorough, scholarly investigation into what exactly happened or written it into one comprehensive account. To anyone who reviewed the evidence—and many journalists and historians had—it was clear that Lee wasn't the only one orchestrating the attack. Some speculated Brigham Young knew about it or even ordered it.

Juanita realized she was in a unique position: She knew how to do historical research. She knew how to write. She already knew people who might have evidence about what happened. And she was one of few people who didn't have an ax to grind for or against the Mormon church. Someone should tell the truth about Mountain Meadows. And no one could tell it the way she could.

In 1945 she got a grant from the Huntington Library in California, which had the original transcripts of John D. Lee's trial, and used part of it to hire others to do her domestic chores while she traveled around the West, looking for sources for the book and other research. She fought for access to the Mormon church archives, which included early documents relating to the massacre.

To write the book, she had to gather information no one had ever compiled. And it wasn't easy. For a long time, Dixie residents had tried to forget the brutal tragedy, and when Juanita started to investigate it, they felt she was reopening old wounds that should stay closed. Why publicize the details of such an ugly event, since doing so could embarrass her own church?

Her resolve to uncover the truth, whatever it may be, took a lot of bravery. She faced ostracism from church leaders (who banned her from publishing any work in official church publications when they found out what she was doing) and even her local congregation. She knew she risked not only disapproval but possibly excommunication, no small threat to a believer. She initially hid some of her fact-finding activities from the church leadership in Salt Lake City, fearing they would try to stop her.

But she persevered, showing the determination that had propelled her all her life.

She hoped her fellow Mormons would see her not as a gadfly but as a sincere member of their congregation. If their faith was as strong as her own, she felt, nothing she wrote could harm it. She wrote to her editor at Stanford University Press: "I do not wish to be excommunicated from my church for many reasons. But if that is the price that I must pay for my intellectual honesty, I shall pay it—I hope without bitterness."

That perspective made her the model for other faithful but questioning Mormon scholars, today as well as in her own time.

The Mountain Meadows Massacre appeared in 1950. Juanita retold the story, saying the local Mormon leadership had initiated the first attack on the convoy. Then, they and their Indian collaborators returned to kill every adult in the Fancher party. She determined that Brigham

Young had probably not known about the massacre in advance and may have tried to prevent it. But she also found that he and others, including his counselor George A. Smith (ironically, St. George's namesake), had inflamed the Mormon militia before the massacre and helped cover up its involvement after the fact.

Juanita also took some of the blame and accompanying shame away from John D. Lee, who she said was unfairly blamed after the event. She wanted everyone to know that the massacre was not just the work of one or even a few crazed men. Rather, it arose from an atmosphere of distrust and vengeance that everyone in the church, not just those in far-flung southern outposts, was responsible for creating. She also told how her own Mormon leaders denied her access to records in an attempt to bury ugly truths.

The book got mostly good reviews from within and outside the Mormon community—though some in the Mormon hierarchy either were angry or refused to talk about it at all. She won praise not so much for her conclusions as her nuanced approach to the story. She wrote with trademark humanity and a sense of narrative, which went a long way toward helping heal, rather than inflame, old wounds.

The book made her something of a celebrity throughout the West, and she was a popular speaker for all kinds of audiences, retelling the details of her book and her own part in investigating it. She returned to teaching at Dixie and continued writing freelance articles.

At any given time she was working on many things at once. She edited John D. Lee's diaries for publication and then wrote a detailed biography of him, reminding the world that before he was blamed and exiled for the massacre, he had been a respected and influential explorer, pioneer, healer, and leader. She was thrilled and his descendants vindicated when his church membership was posthumously reinstated.

All this time she continued to run a household and help her children with everything from housing to cars to education. She and Will were a cheerful, hardworking team with many friends and a packed social life. They loved hosting friends, family, or even casual acquaintances, many of whom shared Juanita's interest in history.

Juanita had a vast network of friends and colleagues, including many of the West's foremost historians. By the 1950s and 1960s, she was the center of a circle of Mormon scholars who openly questioned certain church decisions, past and present. They hoped the church wouldn't excommunicate them for their efforts, but some of them eventually were forced to leave it. Juanita feared she would be but never was; maybe her decades of service to the church outweighed her criticisms of it. She felt telling the truth was her highest calling. She was also just never very good at bowing to authority.

As well as her work with the Utah Historical Society, which spanned several decades, she was a member of the Utah Folklore Society. In 1964 Utah State University awarded Juanita an honorary doctorate degree. The College of Southern Utah and the University of Utah would also award her honorary degrees.

In 1965 she won praise for her work on editing the diaries of Hosea Stout, an early Mormon convert and eventual speaker of the Utah territorial legislature who was part of or close to many significant events in the church's history. She acted as a reader and editor for several other writers' books, including Wallace Stegner's *The Gathering of Zion*. Throughout her life she collected diaries of as many southern Utah settlers as she could, typing them up and giving the originals back to their families.

Juanita and Will kept busy well into old age, working on one of their houses, traveling, and socializing. Living in St. George but still doing a lot of work in Salt Lake City, Juanita took night buses back and forth to save time. She didn't get a driver's license until she was seventy-one, when Will could no longer drive. He died in 1970. Shortly thereafter, tired of the commute, Juanita moved to Salt Lake City.

By the late 1970s Juanita had started suffering from memory loss—much to her frustration. Over the next ten years, her dementia worsened, and she went to live in a nursing home, where she died in 1989.

Juanita Brooks closed the circle that began with early settlers like Patty Bartlett Sessions and Eliza R. Snow. She explored the faith that brought her forebears to Utah, and explained it to those who had come for other reasons. Her work was a sign of hope for better relations between the state's Mormon residents and "gentiles." She shaped the way people in Utah see their history and helped start a dialogue about history that continues today—as she felt it should.

HELEN PAPANIKOLAS

(1917–2004)

CHRONICLER OF COMMUNITIES

In the communal backyard, the dirt shiny and smooth from the soap and lye of wash thrown over it, boys with grimy fingers played marbles; girls made dolls out of clothespins and scraps of gingham. "Andy-I-Over," the older boys called and threw balls over the roofs of houses to each other. The mothers hung up their wash on clotheslines stretched between privies—my father's long underwear had a rust spot in the middle from the gun he kept behind his belt. The mothers spoke a special language: "Go-a-Gringolga, tell-a im rossa warra an-a glickerina"—Go to Greenhalgh and ask him for rose water and glycerine. Ashamed and defiant, I grimaced at passing Mormon and other American children who laughed at the mothers, and with wonderful fear I watched the boys in our row and the flaxen-haired Mormons throw rocks at each other.

"Dirty foreigners, go back where you came from!"

This vivid description of a memory from her childhood in a bustling Utah mining town is typical of the way Helen Papanikolas wrote about Utah's immigrant communities. Her drive to share their stories fueled her prolific writing about Utah's lesser-known cultures. She shone through all the other lives she brought to light.

As late as the 1950s, what most people knew about history, culture, and folklore in Utah focused on the stories of Latter-day Saint pioneers and the white Catholic and Protestant arrivals who started moving to Utah soon after they did.

Helen was part of a new breed of writer who combined history with sociology and economics. She was interested in uncovering the lives of everyday people from all kinds of backgrounds, including those who had not been fully represented before.

She focused particularly on the Greek community—her own—but her overarching interest was in giving new light and life to the previously untold stories within all of Utah's communities. And she told them artfully, with witty, lively, brisk prose.

Her writing made it easy to imagine what life was like for her subjects. She wrote of Greeks boarding ships bound for America: "They stood on the crowded lower decks with hope and anxiety, hope for a new life, anxiety that they would be turned back by officials at Ellis Island who every day rejected thousands of immigrants."

In her typically flowing prose, she described the journey from the East Coast to Utah. "Greeks without countrymen already employed in Utah worked their way across the country laying rails over the prairies, building roads, digging sewers, disposing of offal in slaughterhouses, and clearing land of sagebrush. They rode freights, munching bread and dried beans, trying to learn a few words of the new language from small, gilt-edged, Greek-English dictionaries bought in New York and Chicago. They climbed onto wrong freight cars, their food giving out, always alert for railroad detectives their countrymen had warned them against. They hid from town officials who would charge them a three-dollar head tax and jail them if they could not pay it. They were stunned by the hate of Americans. 'The scum of Europe,' 'depraved, brutal foreigners' they were called in print, taunted and jeered when they asked for work."

Like all the best historians, she went straight to the source—or if that wasn't possible, at least as close as she could get. She interviewed people who lived in the communities that interested her, sought out their ancestors' diaries, and combed through government records.

Helen was, herself, the child of immigrants. Her Greek mother grew up in the bustling city of Constantinople (now Istanbul), Turkey, surrounded by people from many countries and of many ethnicities. When Turkey and Greece went to war in 1912, "my mother had nowhere to go but to America—the sanctuary for the world's dispossessed."

Her father came from Greece to the United States to find work, as so many did at the time. He held a variety of jobs, eventually opening a successful grocery store in the mining town of Helper in east-central Utah. He judged people, Helen later recalled, by their *filotimo*—a Greek term that encapsulates ideas of respect for self and others based on their intrinsic character—not their background or economic circumstances.

Helen Zeese was born June 29, 1917, in the hamlet of Cameron in Carbon County. Helper, the nearby town where she grew up, was an ethnically diverse settlement in the middle of Utah's coal-mining country (the name Helper comes from the "helper" engines that helped coal-filled trains climb the steep slopes surrounding the town). By the early twentieth century, a survey counted twenty-seven languages spoken there. Many who toiled in the mines came from southern and eastern Europe. Others were of Asian descent.

As a young child, Helen attended Greek school, as many children of Greek immigrants did, in an enclave called "Greek Town" (there were similar enclaves for African Americans, immigrants from Italy and Japan, and other minorities). But she also mingled with children from manifold backgrounds in regular school and at the local YMCA, where she and her friends delighted in finding a library of books they could borrow. The train tracks brought a stream of interesting people through their town.

This upbringing, filled with so many languages, beliefs, songs, and tales, built Helen's lifelong sympathy for people who were not exactly like her. She once said, "The destinies of life have made me fortunate. I never had to unlearn prejudice."

The family moved to Salt Lake City, where Helen's father was expanding his business, and she attended East High. Though they had moved from a small town to a big city, her parents, like many immigrants, stuck to many traditions handed down for generations. Helen attended the Greek Orthodox church and socialized largely within the Greek community. But she longed to explore the world beyond it.

Helen went to the University of Utah, graduating with honors. She had wanted to go into science or medicine, and she worked for two years as a medical technologist. But her experience editing the college literary magazine *Pen* helped her decide to switch to writing as a career. "I studied bacteriology. In those days, we didn't have aptitude tests, or I would have known better," she later said.

Still, she put her training to work, bringing a scientist's careful eye for accuracy and data to her historical research.

She married businessman Nick Papanikolas, also a child of Greek immigrants, in 1941. They had two children, Zeese and Thalia, and for a few years she primarily focused on raising them. As a woman from a traditional background, she wanted to both honor and break away from those traditions—including the one that said women shouldn't work outside their homes. She researched and wrote on her own time, at night, until the Utah State Historical Society approached her about writing a history of Greek immigrants in the mining area where she grew up.

In 1954, she published "The Greeks of Carbon County" in the *Utah Historical Quarterly*. It was the first of innumerable contributions she would make to the state's understanding of its people's history, traditions, and folklore. It was also the beginning of a long relationship between Helen and the Utah State Historical Society.

For the article, she interviewed elderly Greek Americans, asking to record their memories. "I'm glad I did, because they began dying afterwards," she later recalled. She knew that if no one recorded the old generations' stories, their memories would die along with them.

Helen Papanikolas's passion for learning about Utah's many ethnic groups led her to a long career uncovering previously untold stories. Used by permission, Utah State Historical Society

Over the next fifty years, she would go on to research and publish dozens of articles as well as both fiction and nonfiction books.

The Peoples of Utah, for which she served as editor and wrote the introduction, exemplifies her contribution to expanding access to more diverse stories. Published by the Utah State Historical Society in honor of the United States bicentennial in 1976, the book is about the many ethnicities that made, and are still making, the state into a vibrant quilt of cultures.

The history of Utah's British and northern European immigrants had been well told by the time Helen arrived on the scene, partly because they were more likely to record their own stories and partly because history is often told by those in power. But while stories of a handful of figures from the state's lesser-known ethnic groups had always circulated, for the most part, minorities were placed in a sort of "Other" category.

As the editor of *The Peoples of Utah*, Helen made sure that each of the book's chapters was crafted by someone qualified by knowledge of and ties to the community in question. As she often did when she was working on a project, she stayed up late into the night reading about the book's topics to make sure she understood them fully. She worked with the authors, some of whom were not professional writers, to craft their chapters.

Even as she worked to shed light on underrepresented communities, Helen didn't see the story of Utah as one of "us" (not Mormon) versus "them" (Mormon). She gave the state's "peculiar people" the same care and consideration as she did any subject. She wrote about the larger social, political, and economic issues that helped drive Mormon settlers from their places of origin to the deserts of Utah—just as similar issues would drive later waves of "gentiles."

She appreciated the Mormons' tendency to keep journals, which would later become a fertile source for historians like her. "The past is there for us on fragile brown pages, in terse sentences—often of great beauty from writers with little education," she wrote, her reverence for this gift evident.

But she also wrote about the way "gentile" arrivals disrupted Brigham Young's theocratic vision almost immediately. From fur trappers to merchants to miners to the military, newcomers made their homes in the Mormon Zion for their own reasons. Utah's population more than doubled from 1860 to 1870, and the state added nearly 100,000 people between 1900 and 1910 as the population swelled to about 373,000.

Young had emphasized the importance of farming, but someone needed to do all the additional dirty work of building a modern civilization. The railroad, along with mining and building trades, brought a spectrum of workers to Utah, including immigrants from Europe, China, and Japan.

"They had been impelled into Mormon country not by the grand vision of the pioneers but by coincidence: by meeting a labor agent who was recruiting gangs for Utah mines, section gangs, mills, and smelters; by receiving a letter from a brother or cousin in a Carbon County or Bingham Canyon mining camp; by merely jumping off a freight train and finding themselves in a place called Utah," Helen wrote in *The Peoples of Utah.*

Their lives were often precarious. Having left their homes in hopes of escaping poverty, they often had little beyond the clothes on their backs when they arrived. Few had much schooling in their own languages, let alone English. Lacking financial support, they took whatever jobs they could, often working under difficult or even dangerous situations.

Groups from various origins sometimes battled for resources against one another or against the Mormon majority. Other times, they joined forces in interesting ways—Chinese workers learned the Ute language as they lived amid the tribe, for example. The Greeks often became friends with the Japanese immigrants employed as their bosses on railroad construction gangs, joining them for card games. Various Orthodox Christian faiths would worship in the same building.

Helen was interested in finding out as much as she could about them, meticulously combing through census and labor agents' records to find out exactly who was in Utah and when—and, if she could decipher it, why. She was interested in people not only as research subjects but as people. And she wanted people from the communities she wrote about to be able to see themselves in her writing.

Helen's interests in Utah's varied cultures ranged to every corner of the state. She elevated stories of Chinese railroad workers in northern Utah, Paiutes in southern Utah, and miners to the east and west.

She was most familiar with the area where she grew up: the coal-mining fields of eastern Utah. Poverty, disease, and war sent eastern and southern Europeans fleeing to America just as Utah's need for manual labor ramped up. Men crowded into mining camps, often in remote mountain settings. The few women who arrived were either brides brought from the "old country" or working in the few jobs available to them, mostly prostitution.

Those who were neither Mormon nor Protestant—the two dominant religions in much of Utah—raised suspicion. "Foreigners" weren't supposed to marry into the dominant cultures, which preferred to keep them at arm's length. Immigrants from southern Europe were accused of being lazy drunks, Bolsheviks, or anarchists, especially after they joined strikes and other labor movements. A newspaper article in 1922 said, "Hundreds of Red-Blooded American Men with Families want to Know why they Have to Submit to the Blatant Lawlessness Effrontry of South European Domination."

Helen's own memories informed her research. She remembered labor unrest and mine disasters that killed dozens of men during her childhood. She remembered the things people said about the Greeks, Italians, and African Americans in Helper. She remembered the rise of the Ku Klux Klan in the 1920s, its members living among the people they reviled.

The circumstances of newly arrived Greeks, in many ways, embodied those of many seeking better lives in America at the time. In 1970, the *Utah Historical Quarterly* devoted an entire issue to Helen's writing about Greek immigrants, calling it *Toil and Rage in a New Land.*

Upheavals in the late nineteenth and early twentieth centuries led Greeks to send their sons to America in hopes of rescuing the families' fortunes. Helen wrote, "The young at the turn of the century sat in village squares and in coffeehouses listening to priests reading letters from *Ameriki* and gazing at photographs of former villagers dressed in

American finery. Work was everywhere, the letters said, especially on the sidhero dhrames ('rail lines')."

Eventually, Greeks became one of the largest minorities in many Utah mining towns. Once men had steady jobs, they began sending for brides, who sometimes came with sisters or friends in tow.

Women mothered many children and ran boardinghouses where they looked after single men. Helen wrote about one Greek woman who became an important figure in the lives of many Utah residents from eastern and southern Europe: Georgia Lathouris Mageras, or "Magerou," a locally renowned folk healer and midwife. "Regularly pregnant herself, she delivered a generation of babies, then another, and another until she spent over sixty years at her calling," Helen wrote.

Whatever group she researched, she made sure to delve into what the women were doing. "Mormon women," she wrote, "carried added burdens: polygamy and their men's long absences on missions left them to colonize and to raise families alone." When she wrote about the Ute tribe, she focused on Chipeta, a respected wife of Chief Ouray who negotiated with the U.S. government on behalf of her people in the late nineteenth century.

Helen nurtured those who wanted to tell the stories of their communities, especially researchers from underrepresented backgrounds. One of them was Alice Kasai, who wrote about Utahns of Japanese descent. Japanese families fully participated in local life before many of them were summarily detained in internment camps during World War II—even as some of their children volunteered to serve in the U.S. military. After the war, many Japanese families remained, rebuilding their lives in Utah.

Kasai, herself a remarkable woman, supported her husband and other Japanese Americans interned in camps during World War II. She and Helen cowrote the "Japanese Life in Utah" chapter of *The Peoples of Utah.*

As well as history, Helen wrote about folklore in its many forms—folk songs, folktales, and folk healing—traditions that generations often brought from the "old country" and carried on after they arrived, sharing them with people from other backgrounds as they mingled in mining settlements.

Of the Greek immigrants, Helen wrote: "Folk cures for fevers, for the dread *pounta*—pneumonia—and croup, judicious advice on who was best for dispelling the evil eye—Barba Yiannis, Uncle John Diamanti, the favorite—and 'putting meat on children's bones' were the hysterical concerns of mothers whose wedding pictures showed them thin, even scrawny, but who had become heavy in America where a person could eat meat every day."

Beyond her highly researched historical and cultural accounts, she wrote historical fiction, bringing the same curious but clear-eyed view to the lives of her characters that she did to the lives of the people whose lives she documented. Her fiction includes novels *Rain in the Valley* and *The Time of the Little Black Bird* (winner of the Utah Book Award for Fiction) and two short-story collections. The characters in her stories were often based on people she knew—immigrants who arrived with little and faced turmoil as they built families and legacies in a new land.

"She really wanted to tell the story of Greek immigrants of her generation and even of the generation of her children, to kind of give a complete sense in both history and in fiction of what that was like," her son, Zeese, said in a Utah Women's Walk interview about his mother.

Her research informed her determination to capture the full breadth and color of life in Utah throughout the decades. But she also simply relished what she did. "She had really kind of a wonderful sense of humor. Her sense of the pathos of life, and how hard it is for many people; it didn't quench that. She loved a good story," Zeese said.

Her influence went far beyond her writing itself. After *The Peoples of Utah* was published, Helen founded the Peoples of Utah Institute, dedicated to researching all aspects of Utah life and history and especially to uncovering and sharing first-person stories. It hosted lectures and even put out a calendar listing important dates from the history of various ethnic groups.

She taught at many Utah institutions, including the College of Eastern Utah, Weber State University, and the University of Utah. Her teaching encapsulates her drive to make sure everyone was represented. For their capstone assignments in her "Peoples of Utah" course in the 1970s, she had her students collect the stories of recent immigrants around them, often their own ancestors. She was training them to be chroniclers of the past—but more important, to value the stories of everyday people.

She helped organize library archives with information about many of Utah's ethnic groups. Her collection of research materials at the University of Utah eventually filled many boxes. Spearheaded in part by Helen's work, the university now has an extensive collection of oral histories, what the library calls "verbal snapshots" of life in a particular place and time.

Helen acted as a consultant for documentaries about Utah history, Greek immigrants, labor issues, and conditions in western mining towns. She presented papers and lectures around the country and internationally. In 1984, the University of Utah awarded her an honorary doctorate of humane letters.

A prize in her name is given each year to a university student who writes a notable paper on Utah women's history. She and Nick established scholarships for underserved students at the University of Utah and at the College of Eastern Utah in Price.

By the late 1980s, glaucoma and macular degeneration were affecting Helen's eyesight, but she didn't let that stop her—she simply got bigger computer screens and bought a magnifying glass. There was so much more she wanted to discover, so much more to write.

Helen died in 2004, but the people she mentored carried on her work. As author Miriam B. Murphy, one of those people, wrote, "Her studies and those of others stimulated by her pioneering work broadened the scope of Utah history, which had generally focused on settlement and progress under Mormon direction, and contributed to a fuller understanding of the state's industrial development and its rich cultural heritage."

MAE TIMBIMBOO PARRY

(1919–2007)
A VOICE FOR HER PEOPLE

When she was invited to speak at an event celebrating Idaho during America's much-heralded bicentennial year of 1976, Mae Timbimboo Parry wrote a response letter in which she declined politely—but pointedly. "May all of you have an enjoyable time," she wrote. "I will be thinking of the country where my Northwestern Shoshones were exterminated and humiliated beyond belief."

The event was held not far from the valley, just north of the Utah border, where U.S. troops killed hundreds of Mae's ancestors in 1863. She sent the letter with Newell Hart, an author and historian who did speak at the event. Mae was a key source for his book *The Bear River Massacre*, an attempt to tell the full story of what happened 113 years earlier near where the celebrants were standing.

He read her four-page letter in full, and we can only imagine how the audience felt as Mae's powerful words flowed among them.

She wrote only briefly about the massacre itself, choosing to focus on what life for her people was like before it—a life that would never be the same afterward. In precise, detailed prose, she painted a picture of the Northwestern Band of the Shoshone as they were before the massacre that nearly wiped them out.

"To the Indian the song of the birds was music; the drone of the bee was delightful; the lonely fiddling of the cricket was sweet to the ear," she wrote.

"In memory, he can always recall the hunting of the buffalo, the deer and other animals and fowls, that these creatures were made for his use by the Great Spirit. He can remember that mother earth was created to produce corn and melons for his use. He must try to forget the evil day when men of white crossed the great blue waters and landed on his land. He must remember that his forefathers were friends to the new people and not enemies. He must remember that he gave them a small seat, because he took pity on these strangers, who were running away from religious persecution. He must remember that his forefathers gave then corn and meat. He must forget in return for his kindness he was given poison many times."

Afterward, Newell reported that letter had a positive reception among those gathered to celebrate a state and a country formed on lands where Native Americans once roamed freely. Perhaps, all these years later, they were ready to hear her words.

Mae built her life on the concept of honesty—including the idea that we should look honestly on our past and its effect on the present. As the letter Newell Hart read aloud on Idaho Day exemplifies, she brought the truth to light through the power of her stories.

For far too long, the history of Native Americans was told largely from the perspective of white people. Mae was determined to change that—to bring a Native American voice to the Native American story— and the story of the region at large.

One incident, more than any other, galvanized Mae and others who fought for a more accurate and thorough representation of the Shoshone people in northern Utah: the Bear River Massacre, at what the Shoshone called Boa Ogoi (Big Water), on January 29, 1863.

Long before she told the world about Bear River, she was telling her own family, both near and extended, the stories of their people, as many generations had told them before. "She would sit for hours and tell me stories such as 'How the Coyote Stole Fire' or 'How the Sun Got Its Name,' and then with reverence in her tone she would relate the story of the massacre at Boa Ogoi," recalled her grandson Darren Parry. "There is an old saying that says, 'When an old Indian dies, a library burns.' This was never as true as it was about my grandmother."

Mae Timbimboo was born in 1919, in Washakie, a small Northwestern Shoshone farming village in northern Utah. She was a lively and curious child who spent so much time in the backyard tree house she helped build that her sister would ask, "When is Mae ever going to come down to earth and act like a lady?" Their mother replied, "As long as she's up in the tree, I know where she is."

Mae attended schools where, like many Native people of her generation, she was educated in the white ways of life, including a few years at a residential school for Native Americans in California. She later attended LDS Business College in Salt Lake City. Her lifelong work as a professional secretary and administrator reflected her skills at taking notes, organizing information, and communicating clearly.

She met Grant Morgan Parry when they were children; Grant's father had brought his family when he moved to Washakie to teach the Northwestern Shoshone people. Grant grew to love the Shoshone and, more important, Mae Timbimboo. They were married in 1938 and moved to Clearfield, Utah. She and Grant had five children: Bruce, Brian, Janet, Jean, and Ann. Mae said she never could have accomplished all she did without her family's constant support.

Even as a young girl, she was writing down the stories her elders had told her, using whatever paper she had at hand, getting down every little tidbit she could remember. She especially listened to her grandfather, Yeager (Da boo zee) Timbimboo, who lived through the Bear River Massacre.

Unlike most Americans and even most Utah residents, few of whom had even heard of the tragedy, Mae grew up listening to firsthand accounts about that horrific event. But she also heard stories about the life her people lived before it, and traditional tales explaining how they believed the world worked.

She would often call her grandchildren to sit around her as she told the stories of the Northwestern Shoshone people, the way elders for many generations before her had. "She wasn't like other Grandmothers, who always seemed so old. She was quiet and thoughtful, but you could tell that she had an unbreakable spirit," her grandson Darren Parry recalled. "I remember her black hair that lay wavy across her shoulders, easy yet strong, shining just as her soul did to me. Her dark skin, with its deep creases, told of a life lived hard; a life of giving; a life of loving and caring."

Surrounded by related Shoshone and Goshute bands, the Northwestern Band of the Shoshone moved through what is now Utah, Idaho, and Wyoming, living lightly upon the earth (their traditional name, So-so-goi, means "Those Who Travel on Foot"). They knew which parts of the region would sustain them at any given time of year, and they traveled season to season to find the best resources—roots, seeds, berries, grasses, and whatever game was available.

With pioneer settlers and fortune-seeking miners pouring into and through the Intermountain West, the region's Native Americans had been under pressure for decades by the 1860s.

The Northwestern Shoshone lived beside long-established trails the new arrivals were now using on their way to the West Coast, from the valleys of the Fort Bridger area in what is now Wyoming to the vast open stretches of the Great Basin Desert. As the newcomers passed through, and as Mormon pioneers moved into the well-watered Cache Valley and surrounding areas, once-welcoming Northwestern Shoshones increasingly saw their lives disrupted. The white settlers, and their horses and cattle, ate or destroyed the game and native plants that had long sustained Shoshone people and their livestock in this fragile semidesert environment. By the 1850s, with northern Utah's grasslands and riparian areas depleted by grazing or taken for farming, some Native people were starving.

Latter-day Saint president Brigham Young told his followers that when it came to Native people, it was "manifestly more economical, and less expensive to feed and clothe, than to fight them." But he didn't acknowledge the unintended hardship Mormon settlements forced on them. In his mind, the land was open for settlement—if the Northwestern Shoshone owned this part of Utah, why did they leave it to hunt buffalo every year?—not understanding that permanent land ownership was a foreign idea to the Northwestern Shoshone.

For their part, the Shoshone couldn't understand why the white people would think it acceptable to use up their homeland's scarce resources without adequately compensating them.

"Several Indians were becoming bitter and defensive and were starting to feel that what was theirs was being taken away little by little," Mae wrote in her account "Massacre at Boa Ogoi," which historian Brigham D. Madsen reprinted as part of his authoritative 1985 book on the topic, *The Shoshoni Frontier and the Bear River Massacre.* "They were starting to feel like prisoners in their own country."

To survive, Native people stole cattle, horses, or supplies from both travelers and settlers—which often resulted in violent retaliation by whites, often inflicted by American troops sent to protect settlers.

In January 1863, a judge in Salt Lake City issued a warrant for the Shoshone responsible for a series of deadly clashes with whites. Mae would later say that the scofflaws were not even members of her grandfather's band. "To the white authorities and settlers, Indians were Indians, and there was never any inclination to distinguish between the locals and who came from other bands," she wrote in her cultural history "The Northwestern Shoshone" in the book *A History of Utah's American Indians.*

Colonel Patrick E. Connor and his California Volunteers rode from Camp Douglas in Salt Lake City to a small valley near what is now Franklin, Idaho, just north of the Utah Territory border. For the Northwestern

Shoshone, this spot at the eastern edge of Cache Valley was a special place where they regularly sheltered in winter among protective willows and warming hot springs.

On a frigid, snowy morning, the Northwestern Shoshone people, led by Chiefs Bear Hunter and Sagwitch, awoke to face hundreds of soldiers riding toward them.

Troops surrounded the Shoshone and closed in, killing swiftly and indiscriminately. Many women and children were hit in the gunfire. The Shoshones' arrows and tomahawks did little damage.

Chief Sagwitch was shot through the hand and knocked off his horse, only surviving because he jumped into the icy river, which carried him downstream. Chief Bear Hunter was not so lucky. Knowing he was one of the tribe's leaders, the soldiers brutally tortured and killed him.

The California Volunteers returned to Salt Lake City bearing about two dozen dead soldiers. Meanwhile, the bodies of hundreds of Native people—most of the band—lay scattered across the bloodstained snow. Unable to bury all of their dead, the few survivors threw some of them into the river. The river's shifting course later buried whatever remained in sediment.

The soldiers were lauded for their victory. The remaining Northwestern Shoshone were left to grieve and try to recover on their own.

The Bear River Massacre would be the region's largest, but far from the first or last, tragic encounter between whites and Native people. The government was crushing resistance from Utah's other tribes, moving them to reservations that often lay on inhospitable tracts of land. During the Black Hawk War of the 1860s, Utes fought orders to move from the fertile valleys along the Wasatch Front to the arid Uinta Basin. The Shoshones' relatives, the Goshutes, resisted efforts to push them to the Unita Basin from western Utah.

Months after the Bear River Massacre, Lt. Colonel Christopher "Kit" Carson drove thousands of Navajo people from the Four

Corners area to a reservation in southern New Mexico; the Navajo later returned.

Most of Utah's tribes, including the Northwestern Shoshone, signed treaties that promised aid and a permanent home. The federal government promised to send money in exchange for the rights the Northwestern Shoshone gave up, but it never arrived.

While a reservation was created for the Bannock and other Shoshone bands at Fort Hall in Idaho, the Northwestern Shoshone were left without land of their own. Some joined their cousins at Fort Hall. Sympathetic Mormons helped others settle and begin farming in a desert valley in northern Utah, in what would become the town of Washakie, named for a respected Shoshone chief. It was there that Mae Timbimboo was born in 1919.

For decades, the story of the Bear River Massacre went largely untold outside Shoshone circles, even in history books. A monument near the massacre site was erected in 1932, describing the event as a "battle" with Indians "guilty of hostile attacks on Emigrants and settlers." A plaque the Daughters of Utah Pioneers added in 1953 described it as the result of "attacks by the Indians on the peaceful inhabitants in this vicinity."

Only much later would the white majority begin to rethink what they came to realize was the largest massacre of Native Americans ever to occur in the American West. At least 250, and perhaps as many as 400 or more, died in the Bear River Massacre, making it one of the single deadliest days ever for Native Americans.

Why did the Bear River Massacre receive so little attention? The Civil War was raging, making news out of the West feel less important. Mormons were reluctant to revisit an incident that had them celebrating the deaths of hundreds of Native people, just a few years after the Mountain Meadows Massacre (the *Deseret News* had opined in 1863 that Connor's troops, "with ordinary good luck, will wipe them out if the chiefs named in the writ do not deliver themselves up"). As historian Madsen wrote, "The cavalier unconcern for Indian bodies left on the banks of Bear River reflected the attitude of most whites of the time."

That attitude made it all too easy to misrepresent the massacre as a "battle"—until the Northwestern Shoshone began to insist on telling the other side of the story. Mae Parry was at the forefront of that effort. "After reading accounts of the Bear River Massacre in school textbooks, she couldn't stand it anymore, and she told the real thing," her son Bruce later recalled.

Mae started by telling the story to her own family, went on to telling it to school classes and scholars, and widened her scope to anyone who would listen. By the 1970s, she was collaborating with historians like Newell Hart, patiently giving detailed responses to their many questions.

Their work reflected a national reexamination of America's past when it came to Native Americans. Historians began to publish books and articles that included Native viewpoints. Graduate students included them in theses and dissertations. Mae was one of their favorite sources.

People knew they could trust her to hear and remember their stories—and to retell them truthfully. Friends and family members often stopped by her house, knowing her door was open. Sometimes they would join her in telling the stories of people and events of bygone times. She remembered everything—not only the stories of the elders but also who was related to whom and how, and who lived where when. She had funny, lighthearted stories as well as sad ones, and she laughed and joked often as she told them.

She kept voluminous notes, and whenever a researcher visited to ask questions, she would comb through her papers to pull out more detailed information about the topic at hand. She hoped to someday write her own books, perhaps a series of them—she had enough material. In the words of her grandson Darren Parry, she "ran out of time." He continued her work by compiling her memories and his own learning into his book, *Bear River Massacre: A Shoshone History*.

Mae always credited the massacre's survivors with repeating the story of what happened so that, at least among the Shoshone, it would never be forgotten.

When she told it, she made sure to include their names and particular stories. There was Soquitch (Lot of Buffalo), Chief Sagwitch's eldest son, whose girlfriend was shot off the back of their horse as the couple fled. Yeager Timbimboo, a younger son who would go on to be Mae's grandfather, survived by playing dead.

Anzee chee jumped into the river and hid under an overhanging bank, watching the carnage unfold as she tried to stop the bleeding from her own wounds. "Anzee chee carried the scars from her wounds for the rest of her life," Mae wrote in "Massacre at Boa Ogoi." "She would show them to the young Indian children as she told of the massacre of their people."

Mae insisted that it was, indeed, a massacre, and not a "battle" as most called it then. In "Massacre at Boa Ogoi," Mae wrote that Chief Sagwitch, her grandfather, was hoping to talk peacefully with the soldiers and turn over any Shoshone responsible for the recent incidents. But the Army immediately started firing, and soon "the Indians were being slaughtered like wild rabbits."

She wanted to change how people publicly referred to what happened at Bear River, and the monument at the site was one glaring example. (Her suggested wording: "Colonel P. E. Connor and his California volunteers from Camp Douglas, Utah, all but annihilated the Northwestern Shoshone Tribe.")

By the late 1980s, determined to change how people referred to the site, Mae was pressing officials in Washington, DC, with a deluge of letters. She also wrote articles and spoke to local journalists to gain support for the effort.

Finally, the federal government sent a representative to investigate. He agreed with her assessment. By 1990, the National Park Service dedicated the massacre site as a National Historic Landmark, and the state of Idaho updated its own signage to reflect the name change. Recalling these victories, Mae later said, with typical wry humor, "At least once, an Indian won something."

Mae continued to present the Bear River story even as the constant requests wore on her. Each retelling was traumatic. As she wrote to Newell Hart about her depiction of the massacre, "You will never know how much courage and fortitude it took me to write that account. There were times I had to put the papers away because I could not see for the tears I could not stop from flowing."

Even after decades of telling the story, she said, "It's on my mind every day of my life. I go to bed at night and I dream about those people."

She could never be sure that white writers would represent her, or the Northwestern Shoshone, accurately, or whether white people would even absorb the significance of what she was telling them. After she had contributed so many hours of unpaid labor, the constant requests might have seemed like one more instance of white people taking from Native people without considering the toll their taking imposed.

Mae's life was not all sadness, though—far from it. As much as she mourned the scarred past, she celebrated her people—their determination, culture, craftsmanship, sense of family. She could say exactly where past generations of Northwestern Shoshone would have been at any given time of year and what they would have been doing and eating in that place. She knew, for example, that they gathered in what is now Paradise, Utah, in the fall, because that's where the chokecherries were sweetest.

She told about the people's dances and songs. She knew about their footraces, where men and women competed, with women sometimes winning. She could describe the amazement the Shoshone felt when they saw the dark skin of African American pioneers who moved to Cache Valley.

The Army may have succeeded in humiliating the Shoshone, she wrote—but only temporarily. "The American Indian believing he was a proud race was humbled and put to shame. But like all growing things, he sprang up from the humiliation. He did not hang his head down but he still looked up and forward."

Mae was also an activist—one able to act as an intermediary between the Northwestern Shoshone people and the rest of the world, just as she acted as a collector and sharer of stories. She traveled with other Shoshone to Washington, DC, to testify before the Indian Claims Commission of the U.S. Congress. In 1968, after decades of efforts by members of Shoshone bands including the Northwestern Shoshone, and a century after the treaties of the 1860s, the U.S. government officially determined that the Shoshone were owed compensation for the thirty-eight million acres taken from them.

In 1972, 221 members of the Northwestern Band of the Shoshone were financially compensated for what they and their ancestors lost. By 1987, they had gained federal recognition and set up a governing council. Mae was its first secretary.

She would go on to serve many leadership roles in the Northwestern Shoshone band, including vice-chair and acting chair. She was a member of the Utah Indian Cooperative Council and the White House Council for Indian Tribal Affairs.

During her tenure with the Utah government, she lobbied on behalf of the Native American Graves Protections and Repatriation Act, enacted in 1990. It said that items belonging to Native American people—including their own ancestors' bodies—were officially the property of the Native people themselves and should be returned whenever possible. The law says that human remains of Native people "must at all times be treated with dignity and respect." The bodies of many killed at the Bear River might never be found, but at least other Native people would see more justice.

Mae Parry was a storyteller, activist, and artist who advocated for the Northwestern Band of the Shoshone Nation. Photo courtesy of Darren Parry

Her creativity went beyond her voice; she was a craftswoman and artist whose hands were always busy. Like women in her family before her, she created beautiful beadwork. Visitors would find her in the kitchen with a pile of beads, her fingers working as she talked, colorful jewelry around her neck. She made decorated buckskin gloves, moccasins, or bags for loved ones or for sale at powwows. She had her work featured in art exhibitions throughout Utah, and some pieces are now part of permanent collections.

Mae was also dedicated to her church. Her great-grandfather and grandfather converted to Mormonism, as did many Northwestern Shoshone in the days when the Mormons sent missionaries to preach to them and helped them find a place to settle after the massacre. The family was proud of the fact that the church appointed Mae's father, Moroni, as its first Native American bishop. Even after the church sold the land it had set aside for the band at Washakie in the 1970s, many of the Northwestern Shoshone remained members, their faith unshaken.

One of Mae's proudest achievements was Utah Association of American Mothers as the Utah Mother of the Year. All her life, she said her primary audience was her own children and grandchildren. She was like a mother not only to her own children but to many whose stories needed to be told—and to those who needed to hear them.

When her grandfather recounted his memories to her, he told her that "somebody had to tell this story; somebody had to tell the truth about what the Indians know," she recalled. "And Grandpa says, 'I think you have been picked to fill this mission, that someday you are going to be recognized for telling the story of the massacre of Bear River.'" Toward the end of her life, after sharing the truth with everyone from schoolchildren to Congress, she said, "If I've done anything, I've fulfilled that mission."

Mae Parry died in 2007. Now, her descendants carry on her legacy. Her son Bruce and grandson Darren have both served as executive director of the Northwestern Shoshone Band. The new generations are spearheading the creation of a cultural center at the Bear River site where the band spent so many happy days before the troops' arrival in 1863.

In 2003, the Trust for Public Land bought twenty-two acres in the Bear River valley and deeded it to the Northwestern Band. In 2018, the Northwestern Shoshone bought 550 additional acres. There, they plan to build the Boa Ogoi Cultural & Interpretive Center. They hope to demonstrate their ancestors' traditional ways of life—and tell the band's continuing story.

Mae's descendants credit her both for telling that story so they and the world would know it and for showing them how to bring about change. "She was our tribal historian, story teller, and keeper of the sacred things—but she was a treasure to me," Darren Parry wrote. "She dedicated her whole life to making sure that the story of her people was told."

He wrote: "She set the record straight when it came to our Native American history, but it was also important to her that everyone's point of view was heard and respected. She would often say to me, 'What is your story going to be?'"

BARBARA TOOMER

(1929–2018)

FIGHTER FOR DISABILITY RIGHTS

It was the late 1980s, and Barbara Toomer and her fellow disability rights activists were fed up. The Utah Transit Authority was refusing to install lifts to make its buses accessible for people who, like her, used wheelchairs.

After years of being ignored as they sat on committees and task forces for agencies that made big promises but no progress, the activists were ready for something dramatic. "We'd tried hard for years to work within the system," Barbara later recalled, "so what we finally decided to do was to stop, or at least slow their buses down."

Their nonviolent but direct tactics included "crawl-ons": wheelchair users would climb out of their chairs and then hoist themselves onto buses with their arms as drivers and riders watched, horrified. Barbara described a "crawl-on" as "where you kind of guppy up the stairs and someone throws a wheelchair on, and then you get down to the next stop and you crawl off."

Her daughter, Jennifer Toomer-Cook, recalled watching a "crawl-on" unfold. "The bus stops, the doors open, and this man launches himself out of his wheelchair, falls to the ground, and starts dragging himself, army-crawling," Jennifer said. "He grabs the steps, pulls himself up. . . . It's rush hour, and you're on the bus. What are you going to do?"

Bus drivers looked on, agape. Passengers offered help, but the activists declined. "It was so mortifying and effective and amazing and gutsy," Jennifer said.

When the head of UTA still refused to meet with Barbara and her team, they asked fellow activists from surrounding states to join them.

They needed big numbers to deploy a technique they had used in other places: blocking buses at Salt Lake City's busy intersections.

"There were about thirty-five or forty of us, and we went out on Main Street at five o'clock and stopped every bus in the system," Toomer said. A half hour or so later, the head of UTA finally told them "Okay, you can have your meeting. We'll talk."

The result: because of pressure from the disability community and its allies, Salt Lake City buses were already wheelchair accessible by the time the Americans with Disabilities Act was passed in 1990.

Barbara was a leader among people with disabilities who fought unequal treatment, calling for change and protesting with their bodies to the point that they risked their own health—even their own lives.

She was born Barbara Greenlee in Pasadena, California, in 1929. Her father got a job as a caretaker at the Edgar Rice Burroughs ranch in Tarzana during the Depression, and the family eventually moved to Santa Monica, where Barbara excelled at sports, especially swimming and basketball, in high school.

She went to community college and wanted to go on to UCLA, intending to become a physical education teacher, but her family couldn't afford the tuition. She later wrote: "My mother said, 'You have always acted as though you needed to help people, why don't you try nursing?'"

Helping people would be a priority throughout Barbara's life, as would a desire for justice. She was ready to fight for the underdog and against discrimination from the beginning. Soon after she graduated from nursing school in San Francisco, she questioned why a male nurse's salary was higher than the women's. She had lively political debates with her father; during the McCarthy era of the 1950s, they disagreed over whether one of her community-college instructors should have to sign a loyalty oath. The instructor "gave us reasons why he didn't want to sign, and they seemed reasonable to me. My father and I had a huge argument about that, about how he was a communist and teaching me wrong," Barbara said. "Basically, at that point, I decided there's something wrong somewhere, that there was discrimination going on."

By 1953, she decided to join the Army Nurse Corps. Her father had always been patriotic, but a heart problem kept him from military service, and her sister had joined the U.S. Air Force. After basic training, Barbara was sent to Fort Bragg, North Carolina. There, she met the man who would become her husband: Gerald Ross Toomer (who went by Ross), a captain, West Point grad, and airborne-division parachuter originally from Idaho. They fell in love almost instantly and married quickly.

Barbara took on more and more responsibility, eventually running the hospital's emergency room and then the whole hospital during night shifts as a mere second lieutenant.

The military introduced her to all kinds of people from different backgrounds, broadening her perspective. "I was able to see people as a whole. I didn't look at people from a religious standpoint, I didn't look at them from their ethnic backgrounds," she recalled.

Pregnant with her first child, she left Army service after her two-year duty and went home to California to deliver the baby while Ross was out of the country for work. Barbara later remembered asking about the polio vaccine at the hospital; she was told it had just run out.

After her daughter Jean was born in 1956 and she and Ross were reunited in Kentucky, she asked about the vaccine again and was told there was a shortage—only enough for children. Jean got vaccinated; Barbara didn't.

In September of that year, Barbara developed an intense headache and pain in her back. A doctor confirmed polio, and she went straight to the hospital.

At first, she could barely move her arms or legs. After months of living in the hospital and doing daily physical therapy, she gained upper-body mobility. Ross visited her every day, but most of her friends stayed away.

One day, one of her friends made plans to visit. The nurses helped Barbara get dolled up, doing her hair and painting her nails for this long-awaited special occasion. She waited and waited . . . but the friend never came. Instead, she sent an apologetic note saying she "just couldn't bear to see you that way." So even before Barbara left the hospital, "I had some inkling that I was not welcome everywhere, or that people didn't want to see me."

She was crushed. But later, she thought back to the incident and saw it in a different light. What did the friend mean, "that way"? What was so wrong about the way she was?

Always wanting to be useful, Barbara volunteered to work the front desk at the physical therapy clinic between her treatment sessions, greeting people as they came in.

One of her physical therapists, a Major Dunkle, insisted that in order for Barbara to have as full a life as possible, she would have to start relearning how to do things for herself. On one of her first nights at their house after the hospital started letting her spend weekends at home, Ross helped her clear the dinner table—and then left her alone to do the dishes. Feeling abandoned and sorry for herself, she started to cry.

When she returned to the living room, he asked, "What's wrong?"

"I said, 'You never do anything for me,'" she recalled. "So he kind of held me and said, 'You know, Dunkle said if I do it for you you're never going to do it for yourself, so you're just going to have to grin and bear it because you're going to have to do it yourself.'" Barbara laughed as she told the story. "I was most offended, but you know, he's right. He's absolutely correct. If you have to do it, you will do it and you'll figure out a way to do it." That became one of the grounding philosophies of her life. If you could figure out a way to do it, you did.

In time, Barbara's arms grew strong, and she could pull herself up to standing when she needed to. From the beginning, Ross delighted in devising ways to make their household work for her. He single-handedly engineered gadgets at a time when ready-made adaptive equipment was hard to come by. "Everything was rigged up somehow, in the house. He took pride in it," Jennifer recalled.

Ross was swept out of the Army as part of a downsizing program in 1961 and went to work in the corporate world. While they were living in Minnesota, having had two additional children, James and Jennifer, the couple decided to move back to the West in 1974. By this time, their daughter Jean was an adult and had moved there, and the wide-open spaces appealed to them. It was the part of the country where they felt most at home.

Their marriage was an equal partnership. When the company Ross worked for closed down and Barbara had a job at a nonprofit, he took over some of the child-rearing duties. She remained the consummate mother and homemaker, though, tending her garden, joining the PTA, and leading the local LDS Relief Society.

Barbara cofounded the Utah Independent Living Center (UILC) in 1981 and was elected vice-chair of its board, becoming chair in 1984. The center worked to help people with disabilities to live independently, and for that to happen, policies needed to change. But she quickly learned that when it came to getting things done, informing policy makers about problems wasn't enough.

She pushed harder and harder, experimenting and learning. She would go on to spend much of the next four decades inspiring, leading, and mentoring others in activism. She was part of a wave of disability activists making noise around the world.

Historically, many people with physical, intellectual, or learning disabilities were institutionalized, hospitalized, or otherwise dependent

Barbara Toomer worked cheerfully but tirelessly for the rights of people with disabilities.
Courtesy of the Toomer family

on others. Children with disabilities were often relegated to "special-needs" schools away from their nondisabled peers.

At worst, some people believed disability was the result of a kind of moral failing, as though it was a consequence of someone having done something wrong. And at very worst, they saw disabled people as a problem for society to solve, which it did for much of the twentieth century with incarceration, infantilization, and forced sterilization. People with disabilities were supposed to stay invisible—and the way the world was set up ensured that's the way it was.

As author Fred Pelka wrote, "This isolation was reinforced by the physical infrastructure—streets without curb cuts, buildings without ramps, public transit systems that were virtually impossible for people with mobility or perceptual disabilities to use—so that it was rare even to see a person with such a disability out in public. In this way society's judgment of disability was literally carved in stone."

Blind and deaf Americans started organizing around the turn of the twentieth century, often focusing on employment discrimination. Disabled World War II veterans demanded the full benefits of their service.

But along with other social movements, the disability rights movement really took off amid the 1960s culture of experimentation. Wheelchair user Ed Roberts helped kick it off in 1962 by insisting that he be allowed to attend the University of California, Berkeley. Other students followed, eventually organizing themselves into the "Rolling Quads" and demanding better accommodation. The Center for Independent Living on campus would become a model for future organizations helping people with disabilities to live full lives.

In 1970, Judy Heumann and other activists founded Disabled in Action, a group that pioneered active protest. One of its first actions was to shut down the street in front of President Richard Nixon's New York offices—and thus much of the city—to protest the president's veto of the Rehabilitation Act. When he finally signed it in 1973, the act was the first national law prohibiting discrimination based on disability. Section 504 of the act said that "no otherwise qualified handicapped individual in the United States shall solely on the basis of his handicap, be excluded from the participation, be denied the benefits of, or be subjected to discrimination under any program or activity receiving federal financial assistance."

Passing the law was one thing; implementing it was another. Agencies dragged their feet for years, claiming that it would be too expensive. In 1977, people with disabilities organized sit-ins at offices of the Department of Health, Education, and Welfare, which was tasked with developing the regulations required to implement the law. In San Francisco, aided by other civil rights activists and disabled veterans' groups, people with a broad range of disabilities occupied an office building for twenty-six days. When the San Francisco sit-in hit national news, the government gave in and published the regulations.

This was one of the first of many legislative victories won only after years of pressure from people with disabilities. In the late 1970s, Barbara joined that fight.

A lack of access to public transportation was a huge obstacle for many disabled people. For someone of limited mobility, and especially for those with limited means, transport could make the difference between an isolated life and a full one. They had tried asking agencies to make buses accessible; they had tried suing. In return, they got many empty promises but not much progress.

In 1978, Denver activists, tired of asking the local transportation authority to install lifts on buses, blockaded buses in that city's downtown for two days. The transit authority promised to immediately start making buses more accessible.

Barbara got to know the Denver crew through the Utah Independent Living Center and happily joined forces with them. These were her kind of people.

Inspired by the success in Denver, activists including Barbara formed ADAPT (Americans Disabled for Accessible Public Transit) to advocate for their right to mobility. Their goal: use direct action to force public agencies to make transportation more accessible. Their main target: the American Public Transit Association, a national trade group that lobbied against accessibility requirements.

Barbara and other disability advocates flew to Denver to protest at a meeting of transit officials from across the country.

Debra Mair of UILC recalled, "We stayed at local homes that were only partially accessible, organized for the protest in an old, cold church, arrived the next day at a local Denver hotel, casually filed into a room where transit authorities from across the county were meeting and then; quietly at first, then getting louder and louder, chanted, 'we will ride, WE WILL RIDE.' We were politely, then not so politely, asked to leave, but we surrounded the hotel and continued the chant. What an experience!!!'"

Barbara participated with other ADAPT activists in protests around the country. For people of limited mobility and, often, multiple health issues, protests were dangerous. During one of their Denver protests, Barbara worried that demonstrators would get frostbite from sitting in their wheelchairs for hours out in the cold.

Many were arrested, which often resulted in police having to haul them into jail through a garage or basement because the jail wasn't wheelchair accessible. Sometimes the wheelchairs wouldn't even fit through the jail-cell doors.

As fellow ADAPT activist Mark Johnson recalled, "You pushed. You pushed hard. You didn't just go up to the front door and go limp and say, 'Take me off to jail.' You didn't do that. You went up to the door, you blocked it for a while, and then you handcuffed yourself to it."

Like many protest leaders, Barbara was arrested dozens of times. She went to jail on at least thirty occasions. "Barbara never asked anything of us that she wasn't willing to give herself, but that set an extremely high bar," Jerry Costly of Utah ADAPT later said.

Jennifer Toomer-Cook vividly recalled a time in her childhood when Barbara called from jail. The fact that Barbara was in jail wasn't unusual. But this time, she and her fellow disability rights activists were also on a hunger strike.

"My dad put me on the phone and I said, 'Why are you doing this, Mom? You're gonna die! I don't want you to die,'" Jennifer remembered.

Barbara replied, "Honey, I'm not going to die. And: you don't give in. This is what we do; this is what we fight for. Why would I give in now?"

Like many activists fighting for the rights of people with disabilities, Barbara had a lot of practice at not giving in.

In this case, police had jailed dozens of activists for blocking traffic. Rather than backing down, the protesters had stepped it up a notch. Jennifer recalls Barbara's reasoning: "You've got 150 people in wheelchairs in here, and some of us are pretty medically fragile. Since you won't let us out, you won't talk to us, you won't give us a meeting, we're not going to eat or drink. See how fun *that* is."

A judge soon ordered everyone into the courtroom. Furious, he dropped the charges and said "Get out. Just don't come back."

Every action, every moment of building community, and every success showed people with disabilities that they were not powerless—not when they joined forces and demanded power. "Those of us with disabilities were imbued with a new sense of pride, strength, community and confidence. For the first time, many of us felt proud of who we were. And we understood that our isolation and segregation stemmed from societal policy, not from some personal defects on our part," wrote activist Kitty Cone.

Barbara's time in the military had strengthened her leadership skills, and she could mobilize people as well as any drill sergeant. Her nickname was "Sergeant Grandma," ADAPT's Costly noted, adding wryly, "This wasn't a term of endearment."

She was also organized and persuasive and, like any good leader, appreciated those who followed her lead. She had a saying from her military days: "Treat those who salute you with the greatest respect."

Barbara went to Washington, DC, to lobby for the Americans with Disabilities Act, passed in 1990. The monumental act laid out rights of all people with disabilities, as well as responsibilities for everyone else. It included a provision that required cities across the country to make their public transportation wheelchair accessible.

Even after that, Barbara continued to fight to make sure transportation agencies served the whole community, whether by arguing against fare increases or by making sure people in less affluent communities had the same level of bus service as other parts of town.

Barbara's lifelong philosophy was that "you helped the poor. You helped people with no voice," Jennifer recalled. "You give them voice. You support them. It was always someone less fortunate. And when she became the less fortunate, she was like, 'Well, let me give you a new face of what the less fortunate is and what we aren't.'"

Barbara advocated for everything from curb cuts to accessible bathrooms in public buildings. She fought for better access to health care and signed on as a plaintiff in lawsuits against businesses that didn't comply with the ADA.

She and dozens of others piled into the mayor's office in Salt Lake City to demand that he enforce the ADA; after that, he made sure people with disabilities were consulted when a new public facility was built. They slept on governors' floors so they could not be overlooked.

Over the years, Barbara met with high-ranking state and national officials, including President Clinton.

But she invited all kinds of people into her life, and she was most fond of the world's underdogs. People without health insurance asked her for help with minor medical issues. Women leaving abusive relationships came for support and a shoulder to cry on. Members of the LGBTQ+ community were a frequent presence at her house, giving early and ongoing support to the disability rights movement.

With transportation and accessibility victories under her belt, Barbara turned her efforts to ensuring that people who needed extra help could get it—in the ways that worked best for them. In some ways, the trajectory of her advocacy mirrored what was happening in her own life. She began to focus on championing independent living for people with disabilities in the early 1990s, just as her own health grew more precarious. She had developed post-polio syndrome, which weakened her arms and made it impossible for her to pull herself up out of her wheelchair.

Ongoing transportation issues led Barbara to help found the Disabled Rights Action Committee in 1991. But DRAC was soon working on issues far beyond that scope, connecting people with disabilities with the information and help they needed to live independent lives. Today, it still supports the community, lobbies for better enforcement of anti-discrimination laws, and sues when necessary. It has also joined other groups representing marginalized people to demand better medical care and more affordable housing.

One driving force behind disability activism was the way disabled people had long been treated in institutions, including nursing homes. Barbara, along with ADAPT (which now stands for American Disabled for Attendant Programs Today) and DRAC, pivoted to working to ensure that disabled people could live more independently.

She always had her family by her side, but she knew not everyone had the resources—both internal and external—that she had. Many other disabled people didn't have an alternative to what Barbara called being "committed" to a nursing home. She felt strongly that people affected by disability should be able to decide what was best for them. She fought to give disabled people the tools to be cared for in their homes rather than in institutions, if they so desired.

She liked to say, "We don't help people live with their disabilities; we help people with disabilities live." She wanted disabled people "to really do the things that they want to do, not the things that they are taught to do."

In 1999, the Supreme Court ruled that people couldn't be segregated based on disability. The court said that "institutional placement of persons who can handle and benefit from community settings perpetuates unwarranted assumptions that persons so isolated are incapable of or unworthy of participating in community life" and that "confinement in an institution severely diminishes the everyday life activities of individuals, including family relations, social contacts, work options, economic independence, educational advancement, and cultural enrichment."

It was another boost for people with disabilities—and another law that required a lot of interpretation, education, and enforcement, much of which fell on the shoulders of the disability community. Along with other activists, Barbara dug in to make sure the ruling was enforced. She argued that government-funded health care should pay for the recipient's choice of institutional or home care. If the state was going to pay to house someone in an institution, why couldn't that same money pay for services in that person's own home, if that's what they wanted?

Referring to the famous actor who injured his spinal cord in an accident, Barbara said, "Superman Christopher Reeve had plenty of money, so he had service care. Why can't the poorest of the poor have it, too?"

Life for people with disabilities had come a long way since the days when they were expected to live quiet, isolated, dependent lives. Many organizations honored Barbara for her part in the fight. The Disability Law Center named a fellowship for her. When the local NAACP gave her its Rosa Parks Award in 2017, Barbara joked, "I always felt Mrs. Parks and I have the same goals. She didn't want to move to the back of the bus, and I just wanted to get on the bus."

Barbara Toomer died in 2018. Not surprisingly, in one last act of volunteerism, she donated her body to medical research.

BIBLIOGRAPHY

General references

Alexander, Thomas G. *Utah: The Right Place* (revised and updated edition). Salt Lake City: Gibbs Smith, 2003.

Beecher, Maureen Ursenbach, and Lavinia Fielding Anderson, eds. *Sisters in Spirit: Mormon Women in Historical and Cultural Perspective.* Urbana: University of Illinois Press, 1987.

Better Days 2020: https://www.utahwomenshistory.org/.

Bushman, Claudia L., ed. *Mormon Sisters: Women in Early Utah.* Logan: Utah State University Press, 1997.

Godfrey, Kenneth, Audrey M. Godfrey, and Jill Mulvay Derr. *Women's Voices: An Untold History of the Latter-day Saints, 1830–1900.* Salt Lake City: Deseret Book Company, 1982.

Mountain West Digital Library: http://mwdl.org.

Stegner, Wallace. *Mormon Country.* Lincoln: University of Nebraska Press, 2003.

Utah Digital Newspapers Project: http://digitalnewspapers.org.

Utah State Historical Society: http://history.utah.gov.

Utah State Historical Society's "History to Go" series: http://historytogo.utah.gov.

Utah Women's Walk: https://utahwomenswalk.org/.

Whitley, Colleen, ed. *Worth Their Salt: Notable but Often Unnoted Women of Utah.* Logan: Utah State University Press, 1996.

———. *Worth Their Salt, Too: More Notable but Often Unnoted Women of Utah.* Logan: Utah State University Press, 2000.

Chapter 1: Patty Sessions

Arrington, Chris Rigby, "Pioneer Midwives" in Bushman, Claudia L., ed. *Mormon Sisters: Women in Early Utah.* Logan: Utah State University Press, 1997, p. 43–66.

Black, Susan Easton. "My Heart Is in God" in Smith, Barbara B. and Thatcher, Blythe Darlyn. *Heroines of the Restoration.* Salt Lake City: Bookcraft, 1997, p. 34–45.

Derr, Jill Mulvay. "Strength in Our Union" in Beecher, Maureen Ursenbach and Anderson, Lavinia Fielding, eds. *Sisters in Spirit: Mormon Women in Historical and Cultural Perspective.* Urbana: University of Illinois Press, 1987.

Scadron, Arlene, ed. *On Their Own: Widows and Widowhood in the American Southwest, 1848–1939.* Urbana: University of Illinois Press, 1988.

Smart Donna T., ed. *Mormon Midwife: The 1846–1888 diaries of Patty Bartlett Sessions.* Logan: Utah State University Press, 1997.

Smart, Donna Toland. "Patty Bartlett Sessions: Pioneer Midwife" in Whitley, Colleen, ed., *Worth Their Salt: Notable but Often Unnoted Women of Utah.* Logan: Utah State University Press, 1996.

Chapter 2: Eliza R. Snow

Beecher, Maureen Ursenbach. "Eliza R. Snow" in Bushman, Claudia L., ed. *Mormon Sisters: Women in Early Utah.* Logan: Utah State University Press, 1997, 25–42.

Beecher, Maureen Ursenbach, ed. *The Personal Writings of Eliza Roxcy Snow.* Salt Lake City: University of Utah Press, 1995.

Beecher, Maureen Ursenbach, and Lavinia Fielding Anderson, eds. *Sisters in Spirit: Mormon Women in Historical and Cultural Perspective.* Urbana: University of Illinois Press, 1987.

Derr, Jill Mulvay. "Mrs. Smith Goes to Washington: Eliza R. Snow's Visit to Southern Utah," text of a speech for Juanita Brooks Lecture Series, St. George, Dixie State College, March 24, 2004.

Lieber, Constance, and John Sillito, eds. *Letters from Exile: The Correspondence of Martha Hughes Cannon and Angus M. Cannon, 1868–1888.* Salt Lake City: Signature Books, 1989.

Madsen, Carol Cornwall. "Mormon Women and the Temple" in Beecher, Maureen Ursenbach and Anderson, Lavinia Fielding, eds. *Sisters in Spirit: Mormon Women in Historical and Cultural Perspective.* Urbana: University of Illinois Press, 1987, p. 90.

Peterson, Janet, and LaRene Gaunt. *Elect Ladies: Presidents of the Relief Society.* Salt Lake City: Deseret Book Company, 1990.

Smith, George Albert, et al., "Correspondence of Palestine Tourists: Comprising a Series of Letters by George A. Smith, Lorenzo Snow, Paul A. Schettler, and Eliza R. Snow of Utah." Salt Lake City: *Deseret News,* 1875. (Reprinted by Ayer Company Publishers, Salt Lake City, 1977).

Chapter 3: Jane Manning James

Barrett, Ivan J. *Heroic Mormon Women: True Stories from the Lives of Sixteen Amazing Women in Church History.* American Fork, UT: Covenant Communications, 2000.

Bringhurst, Newell G., and Darron T. Smith. *Black and Mormon.* Champaign: University of Illinois Press, 2004.

Carter, Kate. *The Negro Pioneer.* Salt Lake City: Daughters of Utah Pioneers, 1965.

Embry, Jessie L. *Black Saints in a White Church.* Salt Lake City: Signature Books, 1994.

———. "Speaking for Themselves: LDS Ethnic Groups Oral History Project." *Dialogue* 25 (4) (Winter 1992): p. 99–110.

Gittins, Lita Little. "Wonderful, Unfailing Friend" in Smith, Barbara B. and Thatcher, Blythe Darlyn. *Heroines of the Restoration.* Salt Lake City: Bookcraft, 1997, p. 71–78.

James, Jane E. Manning. *My Life Story, as dictated to Elizabeth J. D. Roundy.* Wilford Woodruff Papers. Historical Department, The Church of Jesus Christ of Latter-day Saints, Salt Lake City, UT. 1893.

Lythgoe, Dennis L. "Negro Slavery in Utah," *Utah Historical Quarterly* 39 (1971): p. 40–54.

Moore, Carrie. "Jane Manning James Comes to Life," *Deseret News,* Aug. 5, 2005.

Newell, Linda King, and Valeen Tippetts Avery. "Jane Manning James: Black Saint, 1847 Pioneer," *Ensign,* Aug. 1979, p. 26.

Smith, Becky Cardon. "Remembering Jane Manning James," *Meridian,* Apr. 1, 2005.

Williams, Van N. *Brothers and Sisters Stand Tall.* Farmington, UT: Williams Communications, 1988.

Wolfinger, Henry J. "A Test of Faith: Jane Elizabeth James and the Origins of the Utah Black Community" in Clark Knowlton, ed., *Social Accommodation in Utah, American West Center Occasional Papers.* Salt Lake City: University of Utah, 1975.

Chapter 4: Emmeline B. Wells

Alexander, Thomas G. "An Experiment in Progressive Legislation," *Utah Historical Quarterly* 38 (Winter 1970).

Beeton, Beverly. *Women Vote in the West: The Woman Suffrage Movement, 1869–1896.* New York: Garland, 1986.

Godfrey, Kenneth, Audrey M. Godfrey, and Jill Mulvay Derr. *Women's Voices: An Untold History of the Latter-day Saints, 1830–1900.* Salt Lake City: Deseret Book Company, 1982.

Hanks, Maxine, ed. *Women and Authority: Re-emerging Mormon Feminism.* Salt Lake City: Signature Books, 1992.

H. H. "Women of the Beehive," *Century,* vol. 28, no. 12 (1890).

Madsen, Carol Cornwall. *An Advocate for Women: The Public Life of Emmeline B. Wells 1870–1920.* Provo, UT: Brigham Young University Press, 2006.

———. "Emmeline B. Wells: A Fine Soul Who Served," *Ensign,* July 2003, p. 16–23.

Newell, Linda K. "Gifts of the Spirit" in Beecher, Maureen Ursenbach and Anderson, Lavinia Fielding, eds. *Sisters in Spirit: Mormon Women in Historical and Cultural Perspective.* Urbana: University of Illinois Press, 1987, p. 128.

Peterson, Janet, and LaRene Gaunt. *Elect Ladies: Presidents of the Relief Society.* Salt Lake City: Deseret Book Company, 1990.

Wells, Emmeline. "Self-Made Women," *Woman's Exponent* 9 (March 1881).

Chapter 5: Cornelia Paddock

Coyner, John McCutchen, ed. *Hand-Book on Mormonism.* Salt Lake City, Chicago, Cincinnati: Hand-Book Publishing Company, 1882.

Froiseth, Jennie Anderson, ed. *The Women of Mormonism; The Story of Polygamy as Told by the Victims Themselves.* Detroit: J.C. Chilton & Co., 1882.

Nichols, Jeffrey. *Prostitution, Polygamy, and Power: Salt Lake City, 1847–1918.* Champaign: University of Illinois Press, 2002.

———. "Woman's Home Association Tried to Help the 'Fallen'" *History Blazer,* Feb. 1995.

Paddock, A. G. (Mrs.) *In the Toils; Or, Martyrs of the Latter Days.* Chicago: Dixon & Shepard, 1879.

———. *The Fate of Madame La Tour: A Tale of Great Salt Lake.* New York: Fords, Howard & Hulbert, 1881.

Utah Methodism Centennial Committee. *The First Century of the Methodist Church in Utah.* Salt Lake City: Utah Methodism Centennial Committee, 1970.

Chapter 6: Ann Eliza Webb Young

Brown, Dee. *The Gentle Tamers: Women of the Old Wild West.* Lincoln, NE: Bison Books, 1968.

Cummings, Amos Jay (compiled and edited by Jerald T. Milanich). *A Remarkable Curiosity: Dispatches from a New York City Journalist's 1873 Railroad Trip Across the American West.* Boulder: University Press of Colorado, 2008.

Gray, Dorothy. *Women of the West.* Lincoln: University of Nebraska Press, 1998.

Nibley, Hugh. *Sounding Brass: Informal studies on the lucrative art of telling stories about Brigham Young and the Mormons.* Salt Lake City: Bookcraft, 1963.

Pond, J. B. *Eccentricities of Genius.* London: Chatto & Windus, 1901.

Young, Ann Eliza Webb. *Wife No 19.* Hartford, CT.: Dustin, Gilman & Co., 1875.

Chapter 7: Dora B. Topham ("Belle London")

Arrington, Leonard J. "The Transcontinental Railroad and Development of the West," *Utah Historical Quarterly* 37 (1969), p. 3.

Barnes, Lyle J. *Ogden's Notorious Two-bit Street 1870-1954.* Master's Thesis, Department of History, Utah State University, 1969.

Hunter, Milton R. *Beneath Ben Lomond's Peak: A History of Weber County 1824-1900.* Salt Lake City: Daughters of Utah Pioneers, 1945.

Layton, Stanford J. *Utah's Lawless Fringe: Stories of True Crime.* Salt Lake City: Signature Books, 2001.

McCormick, John S. "Red Lights in Zion: Salt Lake City's Stockade, 1908-1911," *Utah Historical Quarterly* 50 (1982), p. 168.

Roberts, Richard C., and Richard W. Sadler. *A History of Weber County.* Salt Lake City: Utah State Historical Society, 1997.

Van Valkenburg, Nancy. "Take a tour of ghostly hangouts," Ogden *Standard-Examiner,* Friday, Oct. 17, 2008.

Chapter 8: Martha Hughes Cannon

Abbott, Delia. *Women Legislators of Utah, 1896-1976.* Salt Lake City, Utah Chapter, Order of Women Legislators, 1976.

Cannon, Janath, "Taking the Great Plan into Consideration" in Smith, Barbara B. and Thatcher, Blythe Darlyn, eds. *Heroines of the Restoration*. Salt Lake City: Bookcraft, 1997, p. 242–258.

Crall, Shari Siebers. "Something More: A Biography of Martha Hughes Cannon." Honors thesis, Brigham Young University, 1985.

Lieber, Constance, and John Sillito, eds. *Letters from Exile: The Correspondence of Martha Hughes Cannon and Angus M. Cannon, 1868–1888*. Salt Lake City: Signature Books, 1989.

Shannon, David A. *Beatrice Webb's American Diary, 1898*. Madison: University of Wisconsin Press, 1963.

Chapter 9: Susanna Bransford Emery Holmes Delitch Engalitcheff

Brimhall, Sandra Dawn, and Mark D. Curtis. "The Gardo House: A History of the Mansion and Its Occupants": http://historytogo.utah.gov/utah_chapters/mining _and_railroads/thegardohouse.html.

Dykman, Judy. "Susanna Bransford Engalitcheff (1859–1942): Utah's Silver Queen" in Whitley, Colleen, ed. *Worth Their Salt: Notable but Often Unnoted Women of Utah*. Logan: Utah State University Press, 1996, p. 102–120.

Dykman, Judy, and Whitley, Colleen. *The Silver Queen: Her Royal Highness Suzanne Bransford Emery Holmes Delitch Engalitcheff, 1859–1942*. Logan: Utah State University Press, 1998.

Lester, Margaret D. *Brigham Street*. Salt Lake City: Utah Historical Society, 1980.

McCormick, John S. "Silver in the Beehive State," *Beehive History 16*. Salt Lake City: Utah Historical Society, 1988.

Silver Queen Scrapbook, 1902–1904. Manuscripts Division, J. Willard Marriott Library, University of Utah (MS 634).

Thompson, George A., and Fraser Buck. *Treasure Mountain Home*. Salt Lake City: Dreamgarden Press, 1993.

Utah's Silver Queen: Susanna Egera Bransford Emery Holmes Delitch Engalitcheff Photograph Collection. J. Willard Marriott Library, University of Utah.

Chapter 10: Maude Adams

Adams, Maude. "The One I Knew Least of All," *Ladies Home Journal*, March 1926– May 1927.

Davies, Acton. *Maude Adams*. New York: Frederick A. Stokes Company, 1901.

New York Times. "Mrs. Adams Kiskadden Dies," March 19, 1916.

Patterson, Ada. *Maude Adams: A Biography*. New York: Meyer Bros., 1907.

Robbins, Phyllis. *Maude Adams: An Intimate Portrait*. New York: G.P. Putnam's Sons, 1956.

Vance, Marguerite. *Hear the Distant Applause! Six Great Ladies of the American Theatre.* New York: Dutton, 1963.

Chapter 11: Josie and Ann Bassett

Burton, Doris Karren. *Behind Swinging Doors: Colorful History of Uinta Basin.* Vernal, UT: Uintah County Library, 2001.

Fairview Museum Oral History Project, "Some History of Brown's Park and the Josie Bassett Lamp," Nov. 28, 1980.

McClure, Grace, *The Bassett Women.* Athens: Swallow Press/Ohio University Press, 1989.

Morris, Josie Bassett. "Stories of Old Timers," *Utah Fish and Game Bulletin,* Nov. 1951.

Reeve, W. Paul. "Just Who Was the Outlaw Queen Etta Place?" *History Blazer,* May 1995.

Rutter, Michael. *Wild Bunch Women.* Guilford, CT.: Globe Pequot Press, 2003.

Spafford, Debbie, "Ann Bassett, Queen of the Cattle Rustlers," *Outlaw Trail Journal,* Winter/Spring 1992.

Chapter 12: Reva Beck Bosone

Abbott, Delia. *Women Legislators of Utah, 1896–1976.* Salt Lake City, Utah Chapter, Order of Women Legislators, 1976.

Clopton, Beverly B. *Her Honor, the Judge: the story of Reva Beck Bosone.* Ames: The Iowa State University Press, 1980.

Law Library, "Reva Beck Bosone": http://law.jrank.org/pages/4822/Bosone-Reva-Beck .html.

Stone, Irving, ed. *There Was Light: Autobiography of a University, Berkeley, 1868–1968.* Garden City, NY: Doubleday, 1970.

Walton, Juanita Irva Heath. "Reva Beck Bosone: Legislator, Judge, Congresswoman." Master of Arts thesis, Department of History, University of Utah, 1974.

Chapter 13: Juanita Brooks

Brooks, Juanita. *Quicksand and Cactus: A Memoir of the Southern Mormon Frontier.* Logan: Utah State University Press, 1992.

———. *The Mountain Meadows Massacre* (3rd edition). Norman: University of Oklahoma Press, 1991.

Bush, Laura L. *Faithful Transgressions in the American West: Six Twentieth-Century Mormon Women's Autobiographical Acts.* Logan: Utah State University Press, 2004.

Peterson, Levi S. *Juanita Brooks: Mormon Woman Historian.* Salt Lake City: University of Utah Press, 1988.

Sillito, John, and Susan Staker, eds. *Mormon Mavericks: Essays on Dissenters.* Salt Lake City: Signature Books, 2002.

Chapter 14: Helen Papanikolas

Lythgoe, Dennis. "Utah Writer Draws on Rich Heritage." *Deseret News*, February 20, 2000.

Murphy, Miriam B. "Helen Zeese Papanikolas. In *Utah History Encyclopedia*, edited by Allan Kent Powell. Media Solutions, University of Utah Office of Information Technology, 1996–1998. media.utah.edu/UHE/p/PAPANIKOLAS.html.

Notarianni, Philip F. "The Study of Ethnic Folklore in Utah." *Utah Folklife Newsletter* 22, no. 3 (Fall 1988): 2–7.

Orchard, Heidi. "Helen Zeese Papanikolas." Utah Humanities: Utah Stories from *The Beehive Archive*. May 18, 2012. Accessed January 14, 2022. utahhumanities.org /stories/items/show/226.

Papanikolas, Helen. "Ethnic Women, 1900–1940." In *Women in Utah History: Paradigm or Paradox?*, edited by Linda Thatcher and Patricia Lyn Scott. Logan: Utah State University Press, 2005.

———. "Greek Immigrant Women in the Intermountain West." *Journal of the Hellenic Diaspora* 16, no. 4 (1989).

———. *A Greek Odyssey in the American West*. Lincoln: University of Nebraska Press, 1997.

———. *The Peoples of Utah*. Salt Lake City: Utah State Historical Society, 1976.

———. Speech in response to being given the tenth annual Brotherhood Award by the National Conference of Christians and Jews, 1978. J. Willard Marriott Library Special Collections.

———. *Toil and Rage in a New Land: The Greek Immigrants in Utah*. Salt Lake City: Utah State Historical Society, 1970.

Salt Lake Tribune. Helen Papanikolas obituary. November 2, 2004.

Welch, Michele. "Helen Papanikolas." Interview of Zeese Papanikolas. *Legacies: Utah Women's Walk* podcast. June 24, 2021.

Chapter 15: Mae Parry

Barnes, John. "The Struggle to Control the Past: Commemoration, Memory, and the Bear River Massacre of 1863." *Public Historian* 30, no. 1 (February 2008): 81–104.

"*The Bear River Massacre: A Shoshone History*—A Conversation with Darren Parry." *Speak Your Piece* podcast. Utah Department of Heritage and Arts. November 16, 2020. heritage.utah.gov/the-bear-river-massacre-a-shoshone-history-a-conversation -with-darren-parry/.

Boa Ogoi Cultural Interpretive Center. BoaOgoi.org.

Chari, Sangita, and Jaime M. N. Lavallee, eds. *Accomplishing NAGPRA: Perspectives on the Intent, Impact, and Future of the Native American Graves Protection and Repatriation Act*. Corvallis: Oregon State University Press, 2013.

Christensen, Scott R. Interview with Mrs. Mae Timbimboo Parry. March 9, 1988. Utah State University Merrill-Cazier Library, Special Collections and Archives Division.

———. *Sagwitch: Shoshone Chieftain, Mormon Elder, 1822–1887.* Logan: Utah State University Press, 1999.

Fleisher, Kass. *The Bear River Massacre and the Making of History.* New York: State University of New York Press, 2004.

Garr Jaggi, Margaret. Interview with Mae Parry and Helen Timbimboo. Brigham City, Utah. October 17, 2002. Fife Folklore Archives, Utah State University Merrill-Cazier Library, Special Collections and Archives Division.

Hart, Newell. *The Bear River Massacre.* Preston, ID: Cache Valley Newsletter Publishing, 1982.

———. Papers, 1860–1983. Utah State University Merrill-Cazier Library, Special Collections and Archives Division.

Madsen, Brigham D. *The Shoshoni Frontier and the Bear River Massacre.* Salt Lake City: University of Utah Press, 1985.

Madsen, Marley. "Boa Ogoi: Restoring Sacred Land 150 Years after the Bear River Massacre." *Utah State Today,* September 16, 2020.

McGuire, Dean. "Telling Her People's Story: Mae Timbimboo Parry, Matriarch of the Northwestern Band of the Shoshone Nation, 1919–2007." Master's thesis, Utah State University, 2021. All Graduate Theses and Dissertations. digitalcommons .usu.edu/etd/8197.

Moulton, Kristen. "Mourning a Massacre." *Salt Lake Tribune,* January 30, 2003.

Northwestern Band of the Shoshone Nation. nwbshoshone.squarespace.com/.

Parry, Darren. *The Bear River Massacre: A Shoshone History.* Salt Lake City: By Common Consent, 2019.

———. "Voice from the Dust: A Shoshone Perspective on the Bear River Massacre." *BYU Studies Quarterly* 56, no. 3 (2017).

Parry, Mae. "Massacre at Boa Ogoi." 1976. Reprinted in Brigham Madsen, *The Shoshoni Frontier and the Bear River Massacre.* Salt Lake City: University of Utah Press, 1985.

———. "The Northwestern Shoshone." In *History of Utah's American Indians,* edited by Forrest S. Cuch. Salt Lake City: Utah State University Press, 2003.

Schindler, Harold. "The Bear River Massacre: New Historical Evidence." *Utah Historical Quarterly* 67 (Fall 1999): 300–308.

Smith, Christopher. "Army Re-enactors Seek Healing for Bear River Massacre." *Salt Lake Tribune,* January 30, 1999.

Welch, Michele. Interview with Mae Timbimboo Parry. Utah Women's Walk Oral Histories, May 2, 2006. Utah Valley University.

Wright, Sylvia. "The Search Is On for the Site of the Worst Indian Massacre in U.S. History." *Smithsonian,* May 13, 2013.

Chapter 16: Barbara Toomer

"About *Olmstead*." United States Department of Justice, Civil Rights Division. Accessed January 2022. ada.gov/olmstead/olmstead_about.htm.

ADAPT Online History Museum. adaptmuseum.net/.

Associated Press. "Activists Started by Stopping Traffic." *Provo Daily Herald*, July 24, 2000.

"Barbara Greenlee Toomer, West Valley City, Utah." Interview by Becky B. Lloyd, November 7, 2009. Polio Oral History Project, American West Center, University of Utah.

Barbara Toomer autobiography. L. Tom Perry Special Collections, Brigham Young University Archives, 2000.

Cone, Kitty. "Short History of the 504 Sit-in." Disability Rights Education & Defense Fund. DREDF.org.

Costly, Jerry. "Tribute to Barbara Toomer, One of the Founding Members of ADAPT." ADAPT.org. Updated April 26, 2018. https://adapt.org/tribute-to-barbara-toomer-one-of-the-founding-members-of-adapt/.

Deseret News. Barbara Toomer obituary. April 27, 2018.

"DSP History." Berkeley Disabled Students Program. Accessed January 2022. dsp.berkeley.edu/about/dsp-history.

Gehrke, Robert. "Barbara Toomer Was a Relentless Advocate for Fair Treatment for Utah's Disabled and a Role Model for the Rest of Us." *Salt Lake Tribune*, April 25, 2018.

Mair, Debra. "Founding Member of UILC Dies at 88." *Wasatch Scope*, May 2018.

May, Heather. "A Virtuous Circle." *Continuum*, Winter 2018.

McFall, Michael R. "Disabled-Rights Group Calls for Reform." *Deseret News*, July 25, 2009.

Newnham, Nicole, and James LeBrecht, producers. *Crip Camp: A Disability Revolution.* Higher Ground Productions/Netflix, 2020.

"Our Journey." ADAPT.org. Accessed January 2022. https://adapt.org/our-journey/.

Pelka, Fred. *What We Have Done: An Oral History of the Disability Rights Movement.* Amherst: University of Massachusetts Press, 2012.

Toomer, Barbara. "I Was There. . . . Barbara Toomer, Denver 1983." ADAPT.org. Accessed January 2022. https://adapt.org/1983-denver-barbara-toomer/.

Toomer-Cook, Jennifer. Interview by the author. December 20, 2021.

United Press International. "Protests Becomes Wrestling Match." *Provo Daily Herald*, March 21, 1985.

Washington Post. "Disabled Protesters Block Bus at Transit Meeting Site." October 1, 1984. Accessed via ADAPT archives: adaptmuseum.net/gallery/picture.php?/271/category/10.

INDEX

ABOUT THE AUTHOR

Utah native Christy Karras comes from a long line of stubborn pioneer women who crossed plains, married good men, toiled on farms, took low-paying jobs, and generally did whatever it took to help their descendants thrive in the Beehive State.

She has worked as a staff reporter for the *Salt Lake Tribune* and the Associated Press and as an editor for *Wasatch Journal* magazine. She writes about arts, culture, history, travel, and the outdoors for publications including the *Seattle Times*. She also writes motorcycle touring guides with coauthor Stephen Zusy. She divides her time between Utah and the Pacific Northwest and shares adventures with her sweetheart, Bill, and their diabolical pets.